BE A STOCK MARKET MILLIONAIRE

NEERAJ JOSHI

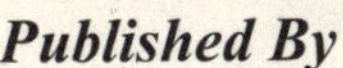

Published By

Invincible Publication Pvt. Ltd.

Published by

Invincible Publication Pvt. Ltd.
201A, SAS Tower, Sector 38, Gurugram – 122003
Phone: +91-124-4034247, +91 9599066061
www.invinciblepublishers.com

Sales: Office No. 4760-61/23 Basement, Pratap Street,
Ansari Road, Daryaganj, Near ICICI Bank - 110002
Phone: +91-11-40198405
Email: invinciblepublishers@gmail.com

This book is a work of fiction. Names, characters, places and incidents are either the product of the author's imagination or are used fictitiously. Any resemblance to real persons, living or dead, or actual events or locations, is purely coincidental and the publisher does not hold responsibility for the same.

First edition – 2023

© Neeraj Joshi

ISBN: 978-93-5886-002-3

All rights reserved.

The moral right of the author has been asserted.

This book or any portion thereof may not be reproduced or used in any manner whatsoever without the express written permission of the author except for the use of brief quotations in a book review of a scholarly journal.

This book is sold subject to the condition that it shall not, by way of trade or otherwise, be lent, resold, hired out, or otherwise circulated, without the publisher's prior consent, in any form of binding or cover other than that in which it is originally published.

Printed at Pearl Print Services Pvt Ltd, Faridabad

Disclaimer

This book is intended to provide general information about the stock market and investing and is not meant to serve as personal financial advice. Investing involves risks, including the potential loss of capital. The strategies and concepts discussed in this book may not be suitable for all individuals or financial situations. The author and the publisher are not responsible for any actions taken as a result of reading this book. It is recommended to consult with a qualified financial advisor or conduct thorough research before making any investment decisions. Past performance of any investment strategies discussed in this book does not guarantee future results. Please invest responsibly.

CONTENTS

ACKNOWLEDGEMENT

I had never thought that I would write a book, but life often surprises us with the unexpected. However, I am not solely responsible for this endeavor; it's the collective effort of all those who knowingly or unknowingly guided me, believed in me, and helped me move forward.

I would like to extend my heartfelt thanks to my parents who guided me through all ups and downs, and encouraging me in all my YouTube and Stock Market endeavors. I am also grateful to my grandparents for their blessings, immense help and support.

But above all,

I want to express my deepest gratitude to my 2.5M YouTube subscribers who trusted me, watched my videos regularly, and showered their unconditional support.

This book wouldn't have been possible without your trust, inputs, and confidence.

Each one of you is incredibly special to me.

Thank you!

Writing a book is a journey that is not traveled alone.

It is with immense gratitude and heartfelt appreciation that I extend my acknowledgments to the many individuals and Invincible Team, who have contributed to the creation and completion of this work.

Introduction

I often compared life to stock market, because there were just too many similarities, be it the quick changes, ups and downs, manic highs and manic lows; but the best similarity that remained struck in mind is that they both go on despite the ups and downs. My life is also one of examples in which stock market played an important role. I must say, I didn't achieve what I dreamt of but I achieved way more than what I dreamt by God's grace. Knowing that it all happened to someone like me, a pretty average student with normal aspirations just like everyone else. I went through the same dilemmas and struggles as everyone does in a humble household in India. The motive behind this book has been to bring out the same struggles and let people know that they can resolve them too.

In Indian households, the foremost aspiration is to have a stable financial system, and the most problems emerge from wrong steps taken while building such a system. There are millions of people out there who hold the potential to mitigate their problems, but are not able to tap into it because of their lack of knowledge. There are three crucial steps to solving financial problems; earn more, save more and invest more. India, today, is one of the best performing economies. If the youth starts investing today, they will be able to lay an efficient financial system for themselves in the future. Hence, this book is all about learning the basics of investing. Because investing is one of the smartest and safest things to do with their money, instead of letting it sit around while inflation eats away at its value. You don't need to be a genius, or have special business knowledge, or secret insider tips. What's important is having a good plan for making decisions and the ability to keep your emotions from derailing that plan.

The goal of this book is to help with picking and carrying out a plan for investing their money. We're not going to spend a lot of time on how to analyze stocks. Instead, we'll focus more on the basic principles of investing and how to think like an investor. Many people believe that the key to successful investing is picking the industries that will grow in the future and then picking the best companies in those industries. For example, smart investors would have realized a long time ago that the computer industry, and companies like IBM, had a lot of potential.

What I want to do is help you avoid big mistakes and come up with a plan you feel good about. I'll talk a lot about how investors think. The biggest problems investors face, and how to resolve them.

"Courage taught me no matter how bad a crisis gets ...

any sound investment will eventually pay off."

— Carlos Slim Helu

CHAPTER 1

THE STORY OF MY LIFE

"The only way to make sense out of change is to plunge into it, move with it, and join the dance."

- Alan Watts

In India, more often than not, there are only a few diverged roads when it comes to making careers. In Indian households, utmost priority always remains a respectable job with a hefty salary. Belonging from a humble household of Dehradun, I often noticed and realized that the next generation, in their prime, tries to fulfil the inadequacies they faced in their childhood. I simply wanted to make big money with a respectable job too. But as simple as it sounds, the complicated it gets. As a result of this peculiar career situation, the prime years of one's life becomes a saga of confusion, existential crisis, transformations, unexpected changes. But fortunately, it all begins to make sense in the long run.

Similarly, my train of aspirations went from all ups and downs, on its way through several stations of aspirations. I find it really fascinating how aspirations change with time. At one age, you don't want to be anything less than a superhero, but by the time we actually come close to making that decision, it's no longer a fairytale, and no less than a nightmare. Although, if your passion persists throughout, everything falls into place eventually. My initial days were similar, being a 7th grade kid, doing everything at his whim, wasn't exactly a difficult job. Studying was not my best forte back then. In fact, I was once saved from repeating a year, when Kalpana Ma'am blessed me with one extra mark in 4th grade. I never thought that I could possibly study better, let alone be a topper. But universe works in mysterious ways, you never know how small of a remark can change someone's approach altogether. While frolicking around, not paying much heed to the quarterly exams and what I scored, a classmate of mine told me, "You're good for nothing, you're stupid." He could say so because he was actually good at studying.

For some reason, what he said, remained with me. For once, I forgot how I was, and only thought of what I wanted to achieve. I simply wanted to surpass him in studies. "Mitochondria is the powerhouse of the cell." "Paper is made from the pulp of trees." I repeated out loud whatever laid before my eyes, again and again, every day. "That must be Neeraj studying," people would always say, on hearing me read aloud near my window or in school corridors. I didn't know any other way of studying. It was the least I could do, come back from school at 3 in noon, and go straight to study.

In all these years, I have come to believe 'what you put out there, eventually, comes back to you,' and so it did. The hard-work paid off, while that classmate scored 376 out of 500, I stood proud with 417. I had beaten him at his own game. Although, I really wanted to show it off and tease him, I managed to resist the urge. Now, there is a catch, once you get into a race, you have to keep up the pace and zeal regardless of small victories over small hurdles. There was no going back to my old ways, hence, I kept up the game, and my marks never plummeted beneath his again.

The time went on, many seasons passed away, as quickly as the games period felt it did. My first aspiration had begun taking its place in my mind and heart. I had the privilege of having numerous army personnel as neighbours. Growing up, I had watched them live their lives, fascinated by their strong persona and steadfast approach to life. To a 7th grader, Army seemed like a dynamic fighter movie that one wished to be a part of, with a salary of 25,000, which sounded like a giant amount to me back then, I had already thought of what life would be like and of all the things I would be able to afford. This aspiration had me keep a short army haircut, telling everyone how I really wished to join the army. Many had already begun referring to me as 'Fauji' (Soldier), and every time someone called me so, my heart would feel a gush of happiness and pride.

Soon, NDA entered the picture. As I entered the 10th grade, I found out about it from a neighbour (2-3 years older than me) who was preparing for the big exam. So then, I got to know that one could also qualify to be an officer in the army and guess what? Their salary was Rs. 70,000 per month. Just like that, my aspiration train began moving towards that station with full steam ahead. I still remember the breaking sound of my brown clay piggy bank, which held enough money to buy a book worth Rs. 560 to prepare for the exam.

Since, NDA was the goal now, I deemed it better to

opt for science in the 11th grade. I believe 11th grade is a crucial phase for a teenager, why? Because you have to let go of a lot of friends, while making new ones. The common mistake that kids or people in general make is not choosing their company wisely. Fortunately, I had found the smartest kid in the class named Pravash, and told him that I am going to sit with him from now on. This decision led to a lifelong friendship. As we became best friends, me and Pravash swam through the deep syllabus of 11th grade. I had finally started to understand his efficient ways of studying and I diligently began to follow the same. On one fine day at school, Pravash told me that he wished to become an engineer. I wondered, if such a smart kid wants to become an engineer, there must be something substantial to it. As I wondered about the same for days, I got to know of a cousin who was also an engineer, earning almost Rs. 1.5 Lakhs per month. My head was spinning now. The train had once again changed its course and towards engineering we had decided to go.

Dear reader, I hope you are keeping up with our train, because I assure you, it is yet to take unexpected turns as everything unfolds. So, as we both kept ourselves immersed in dreams of becoming engineers, soon enough, Pravash had a realization that there were not enough jobs for engineers, hence, he had now decided to choose another diverged road in the woods, which is truly one of the most competitive fields, known as IAS. And now, if Pravash is not into engineer, then how can I be? As we went on to discuss this, he told me about the many perks that an IAS officer gets, including a big home, a car, Rs. 1 Lakh as salary, and most importantly, power. How could I have possibly refused this, so once again I had joined him on the same path.

As we went on to complete our 12th grade, Pravash had suggested that we should apply for Bachelor in science, while we continue our dedicated effort towards studying for IAS examination. We both agreed and went ahead, until I had an idea to pursue BA instead of Bachelor of Science. "I think I want to do BA," my parents could not ignore the tone of conviction in my voice, so they suggested, "That's fine, but don't you think BA.LLB will be a better option." I sighed; it was again time to brainstorm the direction of the train I was sitting in. It was not easy, to choose and commit to one thing which could define the rest of the course of your life. "What if it is a bad decision? But what if it is the best?" the voices in my head kept fighting for some time.

Finally, I had decided to go with BA.LLB, considering that I could also become a judge or practice in court. Although I had made up my mind, I was not able to convince Pravash. Then somehow, all alone, I had managed to apply to colleges and got admitted into one. As I stepped into the vast halls of Law College in Dehradun, grappling with the heavy law books, I had no idea what the universe had in store for me. I had assumed that since I have been good in studies at school, I would be able to make it here as well. But as they say, God has his own ways of breaking delusions. Turns out, I was not exactly the prodigiously intelligent student anymore. Here, I witnessed people with much higher intellect and knowledge. Where I was among the top 10 in school, I was among the last 10 here. My chances of becoming a judge had started to seem bleak now.

And no, I did not change my path again! At least, not yet. I did what I had done in school. I found the smartest kid around, and became his friend. 2014 quickly passed away in studying and I had started to catch up with the intelligent ones. Though most of the time I used to spend studying, there were few moments that went into contemplating the careers of other people around me. On one boring day, I was lying in the grass, amidst the lawn of the campus, right before the office building of the college's owner. As I aimlessly stared at the building, I noticed the owner's huge white car stopped before the building and two huge men, his bodyguards, escorted him into the building, to his office. This triggered a chain of thought. I wondered how educated the owner might be, probably a graduate or not even that, yet he owned such a huge college. At the same time, our professors, who had several degrees, some even had double PHDs, they all worked for someone who is probably just a graduate. The world is truly a strange place, I said to myself.

The aftermath of this ordinary yet significant moment, led to me rethink all the decisions had I ever made. For a while, I was no longer in the present but transported back in time. In the seventh grade, I wanted to enroll in the army because all I could see was the salary of Rs. 25,000. In the 10th grade, I wanted to become an officer because I saw the opportunity of earning Rs. 70,000. In the 11th grade, my train stopped at the station of engineering, and I boarded it because I could see the salary of Rs. 1.5 lakh in my hands. In 12th grade, I resorted to becoming an IAS officer because of its Rs. 1 lakh salary with numerous perks.

A major realization had dawned upon me. I had finally realized that I never wanted to be any of those things. I never wanted to be a soldier, an officer, neither an engineer, nor an IAS officer. I simply wanted to earn the money that came with these jobs. If the college owner could earn so much, despite being a graduate or so, then I could do it too! This realization brought a clarity that I lacked during all those years of changing paths and destinations. It was no longer about becoming someone or taking up a post, I just wanted to earn money. Now, the only question before me was 'How?'

This question kept me up for many days and nights, until one day, I got to know that people can earn from share market too. So, once again, I made up my mind and did what I knew best; study about it. I picked up some books and kept reading until I completely understood the concept. I started watching and reading about the stock market in newspaper and on TV.

I got to know that in order to start investing, one had to open a demat account. Being a beginner, I did not really trust the online system, so I decided to go for an offline one, but I needed Rs.600 to do so. 'How do I get the money?' I wondered for a day or two. Asking my parents for it would only ensure not an account, but a long lecture and life-long taunts! I kept on brainstorming and I finally found a way. My Nana Ji (maternal grandfather) lived nearby. Whenever I used to visit him, he would bless me with Rs. 100 every time. I ended up visiting him 6-7 times that month while going to or coming from college. Eventually, I became rich enough to get an account opened.

Now that I had an account, I had to begin investing, for which I needed required capital. But going to Nana Ji's wouldn't have solved this problem, only a good income source could, something that had no affect on my studies. It took long time until I came across such a source. For almost I year, I did not think about stock market, I mostly studied and gave the semester exams.

In march 2016, I was leaving from a friend's house, named Kuldeep. "Did you know, you could also earn from YouTube?" he said to me very casually. I asked him, 'how?', but he didn't know about it either. So, I went home straight, did some research and watched some videos. It turns out that Kuldeep was right. I thought of making a video, I knew it had to unique, something new, or eye-catching in some manner. Soon, I came across the 'Reverse' app, which was yet to go popular. What the app did was to reverse the videos. So, I made some videos, like breaking a bulb, throwing water, and put them into the app to reverse them, and uploaded them on YouTube. Despite the videos being monetized from day one back then, my videos were not able to gather much views. After a while, the video had made earnings worth $0.001. This meant that it was possible to earn more, I just had to get more views, for which the content had to be somewhat useful or at least funny.

I spent some time thinking about people's problems, and only two things knocked on the door at the end of my pondering. Most people only had two problems or things to the most about; Money and Love. The answer to this question came to me because of college friend named Sanyog. Like most college kids, he had one major problem; he liked a girl but didn't know what to say to her or talk about. He knew I was quite humorous and wrote poetry, so he often asked for my help, how to reply to her messages and so on. When I helped him, he started getting better responses from the girl he liked. This led to me the idea of making such videos. I went home that day, sat down with my phone and an old laptop. Made a Facebook account and created a chat by replying to my own messages, with voice over in the background. This content was unique, hence, it started to gain some traction. I made more videos and uploaded them, fortunately, they went viral. This became a routine. I would attend college in the day and works on the videos at night when everyone used to be asleep. While travelling to college, I would edit and upload the videos, which kept gaining views. Consequently, the day came when I was to check upon my first earning. It was Rs. 19,000. I was undoubtedly happy.

While my YouTube shenanigans continued, I did not lose my grip on stock market, I had continued studying for two years, and finally, I had my first earning to invest. I straightaway invested Rs. 10,000 into the stock market and rest Rs. 5000 were spent on making a website, the rest Rs. 4000 were completely saved. I had not spent one single penny on myself.

Dear reader, you must be assuming that everything went uphill from here, but no, people and their lives are no less volatile than the stock market as I said earlier. Instead working harder in 2017, I ended up getting distracted, and uploading videos became rarer. In 2018, when I got back to consciousness, I was a completely different man, the reasons for which I shall share in another book in future. Now, I was passionate to fulfil my dream more than ever. In order to invest in stock market, I had to gather capital, and YouTube was the only way. On 23rd March 2018, I uploaded a video which vent viral, after which, one or two videos gained immense traction. Within seven days, I had earned 20,000 rupees, which of course, I straightaway invested in stocks.

I had once again started making videos on a regular basis. In May of 2018, I earned Rs. 54,000 thousand. This was a huge amount for me. I was internally screaming at this success, telling myself, "Neeraj Joshi, you finally did it, your time is now!" My confidence had doubled, I was earning on average Rs. 50,000 per month. By the end of 2018, I had curated another website to increase the type of interesting content that I was putting out there. All of it was being admired by the viewers. This significant improvement in my circumstances also led to me build an app, which is available on Playstore even today, with more than 1 million installs and downloads.

Now that I was generating a regular income, I was straightaway investing it or saving it. I neither had any luxurious aspirations, nor did I like spending on myself, and If I had done so, my parent would've gotten suspicious of where I was getting the money from. The only requirement I had was of a phone with a good camera to record videos. I bought one, but I had to lie to my parents about the phone being a gift from my brother. (I do not endorse lying to parents, please refrain from doing so!)

Since 2015 till 2018, I spent the time gradually investing

in stock market while generating stable earnings from YouTube. Tired, sitting on the chair at my table, while staring into the computer, I thought of checking my portfolio to see whether I was becoming a millionaire or not. Observing the speed with which my investment was growing, becoming a millionaire seemed like a distant dream. The reason behind this sedated growth was that I had only invested in large cap stocks, solely based on their stable growth, but these companies were already so gigantic, their scope of growth was gradual yet minimal. I realized that if I were to become a millionaire, I needed to change my approach. After a lot of brainstorming on this issue, I had decided that I needed to start investing in companies which had the potential to grow by multifold times in the future, and simultaneously multiply my investment too. There are numerous companies that we know of today, such huge companies were small at one point of time; the people who had invested in them at that point, ended up becoming millionaires as they grew.

As a result, I had sold almost all the large cap positions that I was holding and started to invest in small cap or mid cap companies. By this time, I had quite in-depth knowledge of the stock market system, I used to carry out all the due diligence before investing in any stock. Even though small companies have a lot of growth potential, more risk is also involved. If a large cap company faces a trouble, it has numerous resources to mitigate it, whereas, if a small cap company faces a trouble, it can either mitigate it or go down with the trouble, leaving you in loss.

Over the time, I had learned the tricks and turns of stock market world, how one could use the basic data as well as economic situations as opportunities to make profits, instead of waiting for 10-20 years for the investment to grow. From this point on, I made huge profits by carefully investing in selected small cap stocks, the process of which shall be explained in the further chapters.

Coming back to my story, in 2018, I had been maintaining several sources of income by now. The only issue that was left to deal with was telling my parents. Ever since the beginning, they had been unaware of the activities I had been doing. "Neeraj is always studying late at night, his room lights are always on", neighbors used to tell my parents. They believed that I had been studying extremely hard to prepare for the upcoming judiciary exams, but the destiny had carved out another path for me, the path of making money.

'Log paise kama kar apne shauk poore karna chahte hain, lekin mera toh shauk hi paise kamaana hai', the quote on my app said. I had been working hard to fulfil this desire of mine with my mind, body and all that I possessed. To gain huge profits in short term was my motto, hence, another idea that knocked on my door was of 'Trading', and soon I started learning and practicing the same. I incurred quite many losses like everybody else, but since the money source was stable and I didn't have to answer anyone for the losses, I continued to trade and increased my proficiency with time.

Now the time had come by end of 2018, when I was ready to make a new YouTube channel. "Neeraj Joshi' was the name of the new channel, which was created to impart knowledge related to the stock market. By 2019, I had graduated while earning a few lakh rupees per month. Thereafter, I had started going to the court and prepare for judiciary for my parent's satisfaction, but going regular to the court had its drawbacks. I was no longer able to completely focus on YouTube or stock market. By that time, I had accumulated 5 years of stock market knowledge. I was earning more than enough, and I had saved a few lakhs in my account. Moreover, I had received a Silver Button from YouTube, which was received at my friend's house, because my parents were still unaware.

It was finally time. I sat with the YouTube silver button in my hands before my parents. They both looked at me intently while I explained everything that I had been up to all these years. After listening to all that I had to say, they only said one thing to me, "No matter what you do, just continue your studies, pursue LLM or Judiciary, you can do the rest side by side."

Since I was earning more than I would've in any other profession, they were satisfied with what I was doing. Soon,

I was enrolled into LLM. Thereafter, I no longer had to hide from my parents to make the videos. 2020 was certainly a good year for me as the videos kept going viral, and my earnings kept going up.

Apart from flourishing on YouTube, the stock market world was almost the opposite. The market had gone down due to the Corona virus pandemic. Fortunately, I was quick to see this as an opportunity to make a profit in the long run. I had bought the shares and left them alone until the pandemic had slowed down. This move resulted in profits that made me the millionaire I am today.

Throughout this journey, which still has a long way to go, has been an eye opener for me. From a young age, we all are consistently told what a gamble stock market is, or how YouTube is not a career at all. Although, I mostly shared my achievements, there were bad days too. But that is exactly what motivated me, knowing I was capable to change the circumstances one way or another, be it through a conventional career or an unusual one.

Through this book, I wish to simplify various myths and complexes that people carry about stock market even today. This book is written with the aim to lay out a roadmap from earning, saving, investing to risk management. Often, stock market related books start with complex strategies and terms. Instead of taking the same approach, I have tried to cover all aspects of building a sustainable financial system with the help of stock market. We are at a point in the economy, where there is lot of scope for exponential growth. If one wishes to make it big, the time to start is now. And if it has been possible for me, it is possible for you too!

CHAPTER : 2

KEYS TO BUILDING A STABLE FINANCIAL SYSTEM

Earn More - Save More - Invest More

When it comes to investing or trading, the foremost issue is money. If you invest less, you get lesser returns, because of which people resort of taking huge loans for the purpose of investing and trading, only to incur losses that they cannot mitigate. Instead of which, one can chose to build a stable financial system with a strong foundation, in which losses can be tolerated and mitigated at bes t, and avoiding a financial ruin. There are a few basic keys or steps to building a stable financial system for oneself, without either of the steps, your entire financial system could collapse or take a severe hit, which otherwise could be avoided. These simple steps are:

- Earn
- Save
- Invest

Even though we've all heard of these simple terms, we seldom follow them diligently. It is crucial to understand that these steps are interdependent. Religiously following them could ensure that you accomplish your financial goals on time. Whereas, avoiding any one of them could pose a threat to your entire wealth system.

EARNING

In India, there has been a predominant belief or practice that a person should have only one job or one business or only one income source. Some professions or jobs are also considered better than the others. But as the professional situations are evolving, there are new ideas, beliefs and practices coming up in our society. One such concept is - Active and Passive income; apart from your 9-5 job, there should be other income sources too. This concept has been spreading like a wildfire. Because one income source means that you're entirely dependent on it, now, in case something happens to this income source, you'll be left with a lot of problems. Hence, an extra source of income only adds to your financial stability. Let's see what active and passive income means:

Active Income : is basically the money earned in exchange for performing a service. It involves actively working and putting in time and effort to generate income. This income is called 'active income' because it requires continuous work. If you stop working, the income usually stops as well. Examples of active income include:

Wages, Salaries, and Tips: This is the most common type of active income where you're paid a fixed amount for the hours you work.

Business Income: If you're running a business, the profit you make from selling your goods or services constitutes active income.

Commissions: Salespeople often earn a commission for the products or services they sell.

Freelancing or Consultancy: If you're offering your skills or expertise to clients on a project-by-project basis, the fees you earn are considered active income.

Other than these income sources, one can opt for tutoring, designing, social media influencing, content creation, YouTube, blogging of different kinds, podcasting, etc.

PASSIVE INCOME: This type of income is earned from activities or investments that require little to no daily effort to maintain. While it may require some initial effort or investment, the goal is to set up a source of income that continues to earn money over time without requiring constant effort or attention. Examples of passive income include:

Investment Income: This includes dividends from stocks, interest from bonds, and rental income from real estate.

Royalties: If you've written a book, produced music, or patented a product, you might earn royalties every time your work is purchased, used, or licensed.

Affiliate Marketing: If you have a popular blog or website, you can earn affiliate income by promoting other people's products.

P2P Lending or Crowdfunding: Online platforms allow you to lend money directly to individuals or small businesses in return for interest payments, providing another source of passive income.

Creating a course or an app: Once you've done the initial work of creating and setting it up, you could potentially continue to sell it and earn income with little additional effort.

SAVING

'You only live once,' one of my friends used to say before taking stupid decisions. I believe we all use this as an excuse to some extent in order to splurge money on unnecessary things all the time. Moreover, in India, the habit of saving money is often linked to images of conservative elders carefully counting coins. But, the new-age "Money Saving" is much more than just gathering money. This fresh perspective sees every rupee as an opportunity. It involves knowing when to spend, when to save, and when to invest. Think about this - if you save just 50 rupees a day by skipping that extra samosa or chai, you could save 18,250 rupees in a year! That's a big saving.

Money Saving also means a "Smart Shopper". One must know the difference between 'needs' and 'wants'. Smart people don't buy things just because they are on sale or because they look nice. They buy things that last long, offer good value, and are really needed. Does this sound difficult to follow? Not really!

Another important aspect of Saving is Budgeting. A budget

helps us keep track of our income and expenses. It shows us where our money is going, which areas need more control, and where we can save more. You don't need complicated apps or spreadsheets. Just start with a simple notebook and pen. There are a few things for which one should take out a significant amount of money and set it aside. These things could involve -

- % of income to be invested securely
- % of income set aside for health or other insurances
- % of income set aside for emergencies
- % of income for your personal expenses
- % of income for family expenses

INVESTING

The most important aspect of your financial journey is the step of investing. This step ensures that the money you've saved, will start working towards multiplying itself. When you start investing, you might not see significant returns immediately. However, over the years, these modest returns can accumulate and compound, leading to substantial growth. The key here is to be patient, consistent, and understand that wealth creation is a gradual process. There are numerous options to invest in, and one can choose keeping in mind their financial goals, risk ability, etc. Check out the below listed avenues of investment opportunities:

Fixed Deposits (FDs): FDs are a popular choice for conservative investors. They provide a fixed return over a specified tenure, ranging from a few months to several years. While they offer lower returns compared to equity investments, they are considered safer and provide guaranteed returns.

Bonds and Debentures: Bonds and debentures offer a fixed rate of return over a specified period. Government bonds, also known as gilt-edged securities, are considered very safe as they are backed by the government. Corporate bonds, issued by companies, come with varying degrees of risk depending on the creditworthiness of the issuing company.

Real Estate: Real estate investments involve buying property for rental income and/or capital appreciation. It is considered a hedge against inflation and provides a tangible asset that can generate steady income. However, real estate can also be illiquid, requires significant investment, and can be subject to market and location-specific risks.

Public Provident Fund (PPF): PPF is a popular long-term investment option due to its attractive tax benefits. The interest earned and the return on the investment upon maturity are tax-free under the Income Tax Act. However, it has a lock-in period of 15 years, making it less liquid than other investment options.

Employee Provident Fund (EPF): EPF is primarily a

retirement benefit scheme, where both the employee and employer contribute a certain percentage of the employee's basic salary every month. The amount accumulated in EPF can provide a substantial corpus on retirement. The interest earned and the amount received on retirement are tax-free, making it an attractive investment option.

National Pension Scheme (NPS): The NPS is a voluntary retirement savings scheme that allows subscribers to contribute regularly in a pension account during their working life. On retirement, subscribers can withdraw a part of the corpus in a lump sum and use the remaining corpus to buy an annuity to secure a regular income after retirement.

Gold: Investing in gold can be an effective hedge against inflation and currency fluctuations. While physical gold remains popular, there are more efficient ways to invest in gold today, like Gold ETFs and sovereign gold bonds, which offer additional advantages such as ease of trading, purity assurance, and tax benefits.

Insurance Policies: Insurance policies provide the dual benefits of protection and savings. Term insurance policies offer a pure risk cover, while others like endowment plans and ULIPs also have a savings/investment element, with a portion of the premium being invested in equities or debts.

Mutual Funds: Mutual funds pool money from multiple investors to invest in a diversified portfolio of stocks, bonds, or other assets. They are managed by professional fund managers who make investment decisions based on research and analysis. Mutual funds can be an efficient way for individual investors to access diversified portfolios and professional management. They can be equity-oriented, debt-oriented, or hybrid, each offering different risk-return trade-offs.

Stocks: Investing in company stocks is a direct way to participate in the potential growth and profits of a company. If the company does well, its share price can increase, and dividends may also be paid out to shareholders. However, stocks are subject to market risk, and the value of stocks can fluctuate significantly. They are ideal for investors who can tolerate higher risk for potentially higher returns. We'll delve deeper into the art of investing in the stock market in the further chapters.

Each of these investment options caters to different needs and risk profiles of investors. It's essential to understand the risk and returns of each option, align it with personal financial goals, and create a diversified portfolio to balance risk and returns. A financial advisor can also provide elaborate guidance tailored to an individual's specific circumstances.

BENEFITS OF INVESTINGS

Think of investing as giving your money a job. Instead of just sitting in a bank, your money could be out there, working hard and making more money for you. It's like having an army of tiny workers - your rupees - earning extra for you. If you don't invest, your money just lounges around while inflation, quietly takes away its value. But when you invest, your money grows, and then that growth makes more money - this is also known as the magic of compounding, which is the biggest benefit of investing.

COMPOUNDING

Also known as the 8th wonder of the world, I believe it's one of the most crucial concepts of the financial world because it governs how your money grows exponentially. Suppose you're a new-age entrepreneur, having started a tech startup with an initial investment of INR 10 Lakhs. Your business sees a growth of 20% in the first year, increasing your investment to INR 12 Lakhs. The following year witnesses another growth of 20%. But here's where the magic happens. This time, it's not just 20% of your initial investment of INR 10 Lakhs, but 20% of the current INR 12 Lakhs. This compounding effect boosts your business to a value of INR 14.4 Lakhs. This is the essence of compounding - reaping benefits not only on your initial investment but also on the returns that your investment has accumulated over time.

Now many of us won't have INR 10 Lakhs to invest instantly, so let's take a more realistic example. Suppose at the very least, you can manage to take out INR 7000 from your income every month, now the annual return rate you can manage to get is 10%. Let's say you deposited this money consistently for years, and never had to take it out because you already had a separate amount of money saved for emergencies or needs. The first image shows that if you keep investing for 10 years, you'll end up with a whopping amount of INR 14,33,914.

Projection for 10 years

Future investment value
₹14,33,914.85

Initial balance
₹0.00

Wealth gain
₹5,93,914.85

Additional deposits
₹8,40,000.00

Percentage (yearly)
10%

the Calculator site

But let's see what happens, if you keep increasing your monthly amount by 10% every year, since your salary increases too. The amount you'll receive at the end of this term is INR 21,14,475.

Projection for 10 years

Future investment value
₹21,14,475.73

Wealth gain
₹7,75,732.09

Initial balance
₹0.00

Additional deposits
₹13,38,743.64

Percentage (yearly)
10%

Is this it? Can we go any further? Let's see what happens if you manage to keep investing for another 4 years. INR 43.71 Lakhs is the amount you'll get! An important thing to note here that just by investing for 4 more years, the compounding doubles the amount that you've earned uptil now.

Projection for 14 years

Future investment value
₹43,71,664.27

Wealth gain
₹20,21,766.07

Initial balance
₹0.00

Additional deposits
₹23,49,898.20

Percentage (yearly)
10%

One important thing about compounding is to understand

that the real magic happens at the end of the entire cycle. Observe the below image, it's a yearly breakdown of the above calculation. As you can see, in the 13th year, the accumulated money was around INR 36 Lakhs, and after a year, the same amount increased by INR 7 Lakhs.

Yearly breakdown

Year	Deposits & Withdrawals	Earnings	Total Deposits & Withdrawals	Accrued Earnings	Balance
0	₹0.00	–	₹0.00	–	**₹0.00**
1	₹84,000.00	₹3,958.98	₹84,000.00	₹3,958.98	**₹87,958.98**
2	₹92,400.00	₹13,565.33	₹1,76,400.00	₹17,524.31	**₹1,93,924.31**
3	₹1,01,640.00	₹25,096.77	₹2,78,040.00	₹42,621.08	**₹3,20,661.08**
4	₹1,11,804.00	₹38,846.80	₹3,89,844.00	₹81,467.88	**₹4,71,311.88**
5	₹1,22,984.40	₹55,148.85	₹5,12,828.40	₹1,36,616.73	**₹6,49,445.13**
6	₹1,35,282.84	₹74,381.36	₹6,48,111.24	₹2,10,998.09	**₹8,59,109.33**
7	₹1,48,811.16	₹96,973.54	₹7,96,922.40	₹3,07,971.64	**₹11,04,894.04**
8	₹1,63,692.24	₹1,23,411.77	₹9,60,614.64	₹4,31,383.40	**₹13,91,998.04**
9	₹1,80,061.44	₹1,54,246.80	₹11,40,676.08	₹5,85,630.21	**₹17,26,306.29**
10	₹1,98,067.56	₹1,90,101.88	₹13,38,743.64	₹7,75,732.09	**₹21,14,475.73**
11	₹2,17,874.28	₹2,31,681.80	₹15,56,617.92	₹10,07,413.89	**₹25,64,031.81**
12	₹2,39,661.72	₹2,79,783.05	₹17,96,279.64	₹12,87,196.95	**₹30,83,476.59**
13	₹2,63,627.88	₹3,35,305.25	₹20,59,907.52	₹16,22,502.20	**₹36,82,409.72**
14	₹2,89,990.68	₹3,99,263.87	₹23,49,898.20	₹20,21,766.07	₹43,71,664.27

You can calculate these amounts by yourself with the help of an online SIP or compounding calculator and see the magic unfold before your eyes. So go ahead, play around with numbers and see what you can do with your money in the long run, or we can say: What your money can do for you!

RULE OF 72

This is an important to tool to calculate how long will the compounding take to double your investment amount. This rule runs parallelly with compounding. Doubling one's money is one of the most common or basic wealth aspiration. It can be done, but it'll take time and patience with a big teaspoon of consistency. So, let's see how this rule can be played with. Suppose you're a shop owner in the bustling city of Mumbai. You've saved up INR 5 Lakhs and decided to put this money in a fixed deposit that gives a return of 6% per year. Using the Rule of 72, we'll divide 72 by 6; the answer is 12. So, your money would take about 12 years to double to INR 10 Lakhs. Let's see a yearly breakdown of this investment.

Yearly breakdown

Year	Interest	Accrued Interest	Balance
0	–	–	₹5,00,000.00
1	₹30,838.91	₹30,838.91	₹5,30,838.91
2	₹32,740.98	₹63,579.89	₹5,63,579.89
3	₹34,760.37	₹98,340.26	₹5,98,340.26
4	₹36,904.32	₹1,35,244.58	₹6,35,244.58
5	₹39,180.50	₹1,74,425.08	₹6,74,425.08
6	₹41,597.06	₹2,16,022.14	₹7,16,022.14
7	₹44,162.68	₹2,60,184.82	₹7,60,184.82
8	₹46,886.54	₹3,07,071.35	₹8,07,071.35
9	₹49,778.40	₹3,56,849.75	₹8,56,849.75
10	₹52,848.62	₹4,09,698.37	₹9,09,698.37
11	₹56,108.20	₹4,65,806.57	₹9,65,806.57
12	₹59,568.84	₹5,25,375.41	₹10,25,375.41

It's important to remember that the Rule of 72 gives you a rough estimate, not an exact number. This rule is quite useful in calculating and setting financial goals, but keep in mind other aspects that this rule cannot calculate at once, instead you can use other rules according to your needs. Below are the several aspects and drawbacks of this rule.

Accuracy: The Rule of 72 is most accurate for interest rates between 6% and 10%. When the rate falls outside this range, particularly for very low or very high rates, the approximation becomes less accurate. For very low rates, the Rule of 70 or even the Rule of 69 might give you a more accurate estimate.

Simple versus Compound Interest: The Rule of 72 is

designed for situations involving compound interest. If you're dealing with simple interest, it will overestimate the time required for your investment to double.

Fluctuating Rates: The Rule of 72 assumes a fixed rate of return. Many real-world investments, however, have returns that can fluctuate significantly from year to year. In such cases, the Rule of 72 might not give an accurate estimate of doubling time.

Continuous Compounding: The Rule of 72 doesn't account for continuous compounding where interest is calculated and added to the account balance infinitely many times. For these scenarios, the Rule of 69.3 is more appropriate, stemming from the mathematics of the natural logarithm.

Effects of Fees and Inflation: The Rule of 72 doesn't take into account investment costs like fees or taxes that can reduce the effective rate of return. It also doesn't consider the eroding effects of inflation on the purchasing power of your investment returns.

RULE OF 69.3

The Rule of 69.3 is a variant of the Rule of 72 and is used for more precise calculations in continuous compounding scenarios, where rule of 72 is not able to produce a more accurate estimation. This rule is based on the natural logarithm of 2, which is approximately 0.693, hence the number 69.3. It's used to determine how long an investment will take to double given a certain interest rate.

Unlike the Rule of 72, which applies to situations where interest is compounded annually or periodically within the year, the Rule of 69.3 applies when interest is compounded continuously. In continuous compounding, interest is calculated and added to the account balance at every possible moment, effectively an infinite number of times.

To use the Rule of 69.3, simply divide 69.3 by the interest rate. For instance, if you have a continuously compounded interest rate of 5%, it would take approximately 69.3 / 5 = 13.86 years for your investment to double. Below is the yearly breakdown of this example with investment worth INR 5,00,000 with a return rate of 5%, which took almost 14 years to double.

Yearly breakdown

Year	Interest	Accrued Interest	Balance
0	–	–	₹5,00,000.00
1	₹25,580.95	₹25,580.95	₹5,25,580.95
2	₹26,889.72	₹52,470.67	₹5,52,470.67
3	₹28,265.45	₹80,736.12	₹5,80,736.12
4	₹29,711.56	₹1,10,447.68	₹6,10,447.68
5	₹31,231.66	₹1,41,679.34	₹6,41,679.34
6	₹32,829.53	₹1,74,508.87	₹6,74,508.87
7	₹34,509.15	₹2,09,018.03	₹7,09,018.03
8	₹36,274.71	₹2,45,292.73	₹7,45,292.73
9	₹38,130.59	₹2,83,423.32	₹7,83,423.32
10	₹40,081.42	₹3,23,504.75	₹8,23,504.75
11	₹42,132.07	₹3,65,636.81	₹8,65,636.81
12	₹44,287.62	₹4,09,924.44	₹9,09,924.44
13	₹46,553.46	₹4,56,477.90	₹9,56,477.90
14	₹44,763.39	₹5,01,241.28	₹10,01,241.28

It's important to note that continuous compounding is a concept more common in mathematical theory than in everyday finance, as most banks and financial institutions compound interest annually, semi-annually, quarterly, or monthly. Still, the Rule of 69.3 serves as a more precise alternative to the Rule of 72 in certain scenarios.

While compounding is a powerful benefit of investing, there are several other advantages that makes investing an attractive financial strategy, such as:

Diversification: Investing allows you to diversify your portfolio, spreading your investments across different asset classes and sectors. This reduces the risk of having all your eggs in one basket. It can help protect your investments from the negative impact of a single investment's poor performance.

Income generation: Investing can provide a steady stream of income through dividends, interest payments, or rental income. Stocks and bonds often pay dividends and interest, respectively, while real estate investments can generate rental income. This additional income can supplement your regular earnings.

Beat inflation: Investing is a way to potentially outpace inflation, which erodes the purchasing power of your money over time. By earning returns on your investments that exceed the rate of inflation, you can preserve and increase the value of your wealth.

Achieve financial goals: Investing can help you reach your financial goals, such as saving for retirement, buying a home, funding education, or starting a business. Over time, the returns on your investments can provide the necessary funds to achieve these objectives.

Ownership and participation: Investing in individual stocks or starting a business can provide opportunities for ownership and participation in companies you believe in.

Now that you've got a handle on investing and know that the stock market can offer big returns, it's time to learn further. In the next chapter, we'll dig into what exactly the stock market is and how it came to be. We'll go on a journey back in time to understand its beginnings and why it matters so much in our world today.

CHAPTER 3

THE STOCK MARKET UNIVERSE

"It's not how much money you make, but how much money you keep, how hard it works for you, and how many generations you keep it for."

- Robert Kiyosaki

Before we start with the tricks and turns of the stock market world, let me take you through the origin of the stock market and the concept of shares or stocks. What we know as NSE, NASDAQ, BSE and NYSE, were a far-fetched dream before 17th century. Investing and trading were done, but at a very primal level. Trading, compared to what we see today, originally meant buying goods at a lower price and later on, selling them when the prices rose. The concept of selling shares and gathering funds for development or growth of the company was introduced or initiated by Dutch East India company, when they decided to sell the shares of their company in order to gather funds for building sea-faring ships to travel to eastern countries for trade and other purposes. What did they mean by issuing shares? This meant selling a piece of ownership to the buyers, in exchange for a price.

Let's understand the concept with the help of a general example. Suppose your friend bought a pizza with 10 pieces, and gave you 2 pieces in exchange for INR 20, now you have ownership over 20% of the entire pizza and the benefits that come with it. Similarly, the company is sharing its ownership with the people who are willing to buy. The money collected by issuing the shares or stocks was then used for the operations or further expansion of the company. If the company generated profits, it meant the price of the piece of ownership or share increased too; which the shareholders could sell and gain profit.

This phenomenon gathered traction with time. The group of initial brokers, who facilitated the stock-related activities between companies, buyers and sellers; set up a stock exchange. Gradually, this phenomenon travelled across seas, and the formation of several stock exchanges took place around the world. In 1698, the London Stock Exchange came to life in the setting of Jonathan's Coffee House. The New York Stock Exchange (NYSE) was born in 1792, under a buttonwood tree. So on and so forth, the phenomenon also travelled to India too in the 1870's. Under the trees lined up on Dalal Street in Mumbai, 22 enterprising brokers gathered. Sat together amidst the noisy cart-pullers, spice sellers, and local townsfolk, they formed the Native Share & Stock Brokers Association. This gathering, marked by the exchange of cotton shares, was to eventually transform into the Bombay Stock Exchange, Asia's oldest stock exchange.

But the Indian market's true coming-of-age story didn't begin until the 1990s. The financial liberalization brought major changes in the country. Soon, the National Stock Exchange (NSE) was established along with laws to regulate the same. The operations of the National Stock Exchange (NSE) started in 1994, armed with a computer trading systems which ignited a new era of modern trading practices in India. In 1995, another milestone was reached as online trading was introduced. Suddenly, the market was not just a physical space; it was now a virtual entity. Today, Globalization and technology have made it more accessible than ever. High-frequency trading, algorithmic trading, and now even trading from the comfort of our own smartphones have become the norm.

Today, we see all the craze about stock market, media is always flooded with talks of NIFTY and Sensex. Have you wondered why? Why is stock market so important? What significant impact did it have on our society?

IMPACT OF STOCK MARKET PHENOMENON

Once upon a time, a company, quite eminent today, had set up its first small plant, manufacturing basic essentials such as ghee, soaps and cooking oil. The plant was set up somewhere in an obscure village of Maharashtra, known as Amalner, a village that spoke of simplicity and austerity, where people had minimal aspirations of living a simple and content life. Thc people of the village had small jobs that helped them to sustain their existence. Nonetheless, would you believe if I told you, the same people of the village are millionaires today? The company mentioned above is none other than Wipro. In the world of tech giants, WIPRO stands out for its humble beginnings, established in 1945 as Western Indian Vegetables Product Limited.

Oblivious of what the future had in store; a few residents

of the said village had bought shares of the small-town producer of everyday goods. Shantilal Jain, one such investor, bought WIPRO shares when the price of the stock was around Rs 100. Despite the share price falling below the intrinsic value and hitting a low of Rs 35 at one point in time, Jain held on to his shares. Today, adjusted for splits and bonuses, Jain's initial investment of few thousand rupees is now worth Rs 5.5 crore. Not just him, Zahoor Ahmed Haji Sheikh Masoom, a retired headmaster, bought five shares in 1947 for Rs 100 each. After several bonuses, stock splits, and some trading, those five shares have turned into 70,000 shares worth over Rs 10 crore. Last but not least, is the story of Mohammad Anwar, nothing short of a miracle.

Anwar and his four siblings spent their early years farming on their family's farmland. However, their lives took an unexpected turn when their father passed away, leading to the division of the land among the brothers. Anwar had decided to sell his share of the land for Rs 80,000. He was only twenty-seven and had a small family with two kids. Now, with this sum of money, Anwar was at a crossroads, contemplating where to invest it. But destiny had something great in store for him, a stockbroker named Satish Shah from the bustling city of Mumbai visited Amalner. His mission was to collect Wipro shares from the villagers. Seeing an opportunity, Anwar offered to help Satish go door-to-door to gather these shares. Satish appreciated Anwar's assistance and as a gesture of thanks, gave him a hundred Wipro shares, each priced at face value of Rs 100. Anwar happily accepted this offer and put Rs 10,000 of his money into these shares. With the remaining money, he started a small trading business.

Incredibly, this small investment of Rs 10,000 would prove to be a game changer for Anwar. Today, a single share of Wipro is worth Rs.265. Anwar's initial batch of shares went through several splits and bonuses over the years, which resulted in a quantity of 2,56,00,000 shares. His shares are worth a staggering Rs.679 crores now. Moreover, he has received dividends totaling Rs.169 crores from Wipro. This means that Anwar turned an investment of Rs.10,000 into an extraordinary Rs 848 crores! Check out the image below to see how his shares grew over time.

Year	Bonus Declared by the Company	Total No. of Anwar's Share
1981	1:1	200
1985	1:1	400
1986	Company split the share to Rs.10	4000
1987	1:1	8000
1989	1:1	16,000
1992	1:1	32,000
1995	1:1	64,000
1997	2:1	1,92,000
1999	Company split the share to Rs.2	9,60,000
2004	2:1	28,80,000
2005	1:1	57,60,000
2010	2:3	96,00,000
2017	1:1	1,92,00,000
2019	1:3	2,56,00,000

While stories of such people in Amalner were unfolding, Infosys and its employees had their fate unravelling as well. The listing of Infosys in 1993 marked a turning point in the Indian corporate world. Not only did they change the way business was done in the country, but Infosys also changed the working culture and environment. In 1993, Infosys' shares opened at ₹ 145 a share, almost a 52% premium on the day of listing. This marked the beginning of Infosys' journey to becoming a global technology giant. It showed other companies in India that wealth creation for employees and shareholders was just as important as profit-making. Employees held 13.6% of shares in 1992, and with the introduction of an employee stock option scheme in subsequent years, many of the company's more than 18,000 employees who held shares became millionaires.

While there are stories of miraculous returns, you must've heard stories of severe losses too. This dichotomy in the financial world of the stock market instilled in us a mixed sense of hope and fear. From these two aspects emerges a question; Is there a better way to navigate through this complex financial world than just clinging onto hope? Is it all gambling at the end of the day or can one actually be in control of their choices? These questions had bothered me too in my early days of the stock market. Undoubtedly, I too had to incur losses in the beginning, but as I kept on gaining deeper insight into this system, I began to figure out a few things over the years as explained in the upcoming chapters.

Now that you know how the stock market originated, and what power does it hold in changing the lives of the people, let's see what the current scenario is, how it works and how you can enter the world of stock market.

CURRENT DAY STOCK MARKET AND PROCEDURES

Let's suppose there is a company valued at 100 crores, and it requires 25 crores for growth and expansion. Taking a loan could prove to be risky. What if the company is not able to increase their profits and, consequently, it is unable to repay the loan? Another way to raise these funds would be selling a portion of the company's ownership. If they sell 25%, they shall receive 25 crores. This ownership is sold in the form of shares; the company just needs to find someone willing to invest such a significant amount.

However, finding someone to invest a large amount might not be easy. For example, if the company were worth 1 lakh crore, 25% of it would amount to 25,000 crores. It would be extremely challenging to find one or two investors willing to put in such a massive sum. But this process could be made easier if many individuals, including common people who wish to invest smaller amounts, could participate. This necessitates a platform where such transactions can occur. That platform is the stock exchange, where Every Public company and its shares are listed. When a company enters the stock market and sells its shares for the first time, it's known as an Initial Public Offering (IPO).

Now you can understand the company's perception behind selling the shares, but why would people buy the ownership of these companies? The answer is; with the funds received from selling ownership shares, the company can grow and expand. Suppose the company's value grows from 100 crores to 200 crores; this growth will also lead to an increase in the price of the shares, which could rise from 25 crores to 50 crores. For instance, if you have bought Rs. 10,000 worth of shares, they would become worth Rs.20,000 if the share price doubles as the company grows.

In the same example, let's say that people bought the shares, and the company has been using the invested money for growth and expansion. Due to some emergencies or personal needs, some of the investors might require their money back. But the company can't give back the money that is already being used, so another way for the investors to recoup their money would be by selling their shares to others. To facilitate this, investors need a platform where they can sell their shares whenever they wish to and get their invested money back in times of need. Now, investors can't sell their shares back to the company, but there might be other people in the market who wish to buy these shares. Since the company and its shares are listed on the stock market, sellers can sell their shares to buyers on the same platform. This entire system is known as the stock market.

Now the question arises, why do we invest in stock market?

Although there are various investment options, as mentioned in the previous chapter, each comes with its own pros and cons. For instance, gold can yield maximum returns of 8-10%, while fixed deposits (FDs) offer a maximum return of around 6-7%. When it comes to investing in real estate, you first need a substantial amount of capital. Thereafter, selling the property cannot be done instantly, and it may take years to find a suitable buyer.

In the case of the stock market, the returns are not fixed. The return solely depends on the performance and worth of the company. For instance, if Company A managed to grow by 28%, its share price would correspondingly increase. Similarly, if Company B only manages to grow by 15%, the share price would increase accordingly. Therefore, returns in the stock market are not fixed and depend on various factors. How to choose a right company that can give substantial returns is the question before us, but before that let's understand how you can begin with opening an account.

How to get a Demat account?

Once you decide that you want to invest in the stock market, the first thing you need to do is open a Demat account. Just as you need a bank account for your money, you need a Demat account for your shares. This account allows you to buy, hold, and sell shares. Due to the digitalization in recent years, every process, from the smallest to the largest, has moved online. Everything can be done with a few clicks on your phone or computer. There are numerous online brokers through which you can open your Demat account in a matter of minutes. Besides that, you can also opt for the offline method, but you'll still have to buy and sell shares online. Moreover, with the offline method, there are full-time brokers who charge higher fees or commissions compared to Online brokerage apps.

How to choose a broker app?

Here's a checklist to consider when choosing a good brokerage app:

1. **Fees and Commissions:**
   - Check if the app charges for trades (stocks, options, ETFs).
   - Look into account maintenance fees, inactivity fees, withdrawal fees etc.
   - Be aware of the pricing structure, if there are different tiers or if certain services come at an additional cost.
2. **Investment Choices:**
   - Does the app offer a broad range of investment options? This can include stocks, ETFs, mutual funds, bonds, options, futures, and more.
3. **Usability and Interface:**

- Is the app user-friendly? Can you easily find what you're looking for?
- Check out the app's design. Is it clean and intuitive?

4. **Mobile Experience:**
   - Is the app available for your mobile device? Is the mobile experience smooth and reliable?
5. **Customer Service:**
   - Look into the app's reputation for customer service. Is it easy to reach out to their support?
   - Is customer support available 24/7, or are there specific hours?
6. **Educational Resources:**
   - Does the app offer educational resources to help you understand investing?
7. **Security:**
   - Look into the app's security measures. Are they using encryption? Is your data safe?
8. **Account Minimum:**
   - Does the app require a minimum balance? Is it feasible for your financial situation?
9. **Ease of Deposits and Withdrawals:**
   - Is it easy to transfer money into and out of the account? Are there any restrictions?
10. **Research Tools and Insights:**
    - Does the app provide tools to conduct research on

stocks? Are there features like analyst ratings, market news, historical performance graphs?

11. Reputation and Regulation:

- Is the brokerage regulated by a trustworthy financial regulatory body?
- Read reviews online and look into any potential legal issues the brokerage may have had.

12. Automatic Investments and Rebalancing:

- Check if the app offers features like automatic contributions or rebalancing.

Once you've chosen a good brokerage app, you can begin the process of opening an account. It's a simple and straightforward process that requires an Aadhar card, Pan card and your bank account details, which are linked for easy access and security. Once the account is created and activated, which usually takes a few hours to a few days, you can proceed to buying and selling shares.

Where to invest?

There are more than 5000 companies listed on the exchange. If you are entirely new to this world, you can start by investing small amounts of money in businesses that you know and understand very well, such as Reliance, TATA, HCL, or ITC, among others. With time and more thorough research, you'll be able to analyze businesses and make sensible decisions about your investments.

Often, beginners make the mistake of investing large chunks of their money in businesses that they have no idea about. The key to being a good investor is to have an owner's mindset. Understand that you're here to buy ownership, and you cannot randomly pick any company. As an owner, you will have to analyze all the necessary information about the business. The process starts with fundamental analysis, which primarily involves understanding the financials of the company. In simple terms, this includes:

- Profits and liabilities
- Debts
- Cash Flow
- Growth Rate
- Scope for expansion in future
- ETC.

You'll be learning about fundamental analysis and much more in the upcoming chapters. Once you understand the basics of a business, you'll have a good idea of the direction of its growth. With this knowledge, you can then decide whether or not you wish to invest in that business.

In order to know more about selecting a perfect brokerage app, you can scan the link below and check out my YouTube video on the same.

Now let's explore the different kinds of stocks available in the market, and how you can discover those hidden gems that can contribute to growing your wealth.

CHAPTER 4

UNVEILING THE HIDDEN GEMS

"Only buy something that you'd be perfectly happy to hold if the market shut down for 10 years."

- Warren Buffet

Indian people are known for their thorough analysis before buying any product, be it electronics or textiles, or household; everything is thoroughly checked and questioned from price to material and even the vendor at times. But when it comes to buying ownership of any such product or company, we shy away from hefty research work, and look to others for tips and suggestions instead. The problem clearly lies in our approach. If I asked you to pick a company you could be the owner of, which one would you choose and on what basis? Would you take the name of the first company that comes to your mind? What if that company is not generating enough profit as much as it is taking on debt or what if the necessity of its products is diminishing with time? Would you like to own it? No, I am sure you won't.

So, how can you select a company that you would want to own? The answer to this question is 'Fundamental Analysis'. But one cannot analyze all the companies listed on the exchange. There are four to five types of stocks, among which you can select according to your financial set up along with the ability to take risks. These types are:

- Penny stocks
- Small cap stocks
- Mid cap stocks
- Large or Blue-Chip stocks

Let's compare the first two in order to understand the capabilities of the companies that fall under these categories.

PENNY STOCKS:

In the vast world of investing, penny stocks appear most tempting, whispering promises of quick riches to unsuspecting investors. These stocks are generally priced below Rs. 10 per share, seemingly attractive due to their low cost. However, it is essential to be cautious, as investing in penny stocks can be a dangerous endeavor.

Penny stocks carry substantial risks and are known for their susceptibility to market manipulation and fraudulent schemes. Their low market capitalization makes them highly volatile, subject to significant price fluctuations driven more by hype than just solid business fundamentals. Undoubtedly, Penny stocks lack the stability and liquidity necessary for sustained growth, more often than not leading the investors to be trapped in a situation of uncertainty and disappointment.

Investors simply assume - if the price of the stock is currently INR 10, it could easily multiply over a period at least two or three times. This misconception leads to a lot of regretful decisions, but at the same, it is not necessary that a company is small if its share is priced below INR 10. Vodafone is one example, even though its market cap is more than 30,000 crores, its share price is currently INR

7.5. If the share price has to be doubled, the company would have to double its market cap to INR 60,000 crores, which is quite difficult. Therefore, we can say the share price does not reflect the size or the market cap of a company.

Let's assume a company is small with a market cap of only INR 17 crores, and its share price is around 1.5 INR. Now, it's not necessary that its share price rise to INR 3 and your money will be doubled. For a share price to increase, it's necessary for the company to be profitable, and it might be possible that the company is not making enough sales or no sales at all.

Let's consider another penny stock known as Khubsurat Ltd. which hasn't made any sales in the past five years, hence, it's almost impossible that its share prices will increase.

Profit & Loss

Standalone Figures in Rs. Crores / View Consolidated

	Mar 2012	Mar 2013	Mar 2014	Mar 2015	Mar 2016	Mar 2017	Mar 2018	Mar 2019	Mar 2020	Mar 2021	Mar 2022	Mar 2023
Sales +	1.98	20.14	13.26	6.69	3.62	2.06	0.00	0.00	0.02	0.00	0.00	0.00
Expenses +	1.93	19.26	14.35	9.33	3.59	2.81	0.39	0.59	0.45	0.45	0.50	0.37
Operating Profit	**0.05**	**0.88**	**-1.09**	**-0.64**	**0.03**	**-0.75**	**-0.39**	**-0.59**	**-0.43**	**-0.45**	**-0.50**	**-0.37**
OPM %	2.53%	4.37%	-8.22%	-7.36%	0.83%	-36.41%			-2,150.00%			
Other Income +	0.60	0.00	1.45	0.91	0.03	0.78	0.42	0.64	0.45	0.46	0.83	0.73
Interest	0.00	0.01	0.00	0.00	0.00	0.00	0.00	0.00	0.00	0.00	0.00	0.00
Depreciation	0.26	0.16	0.10	0.01	0.01	0.01	0.00	0.00	0.00	0.00	0.00	0.00
Profit before tax	**0.67**	**0.71**	**0.26**	**0.26**	**0.05**	**0.02**	**0.03**	**0.05**	**0.02**	**0.01**	**0.33**	**0.36**
Tax %	31.34%	30.99%	30.77%	30.77%	20.00%	0.00%	33.33%	20.00%	50.00%	0.00%	24.24%	25.00%
Net Profit +	**0.46**	**0.49**	**0.18**	**0.19**	**0.04**	**0.02**	**0.02**	**0.04**	**0.01**	**0.01**	**0.24**	**0.27**

Along with this, there is another problem with penny stocks: the liquidity of these companies is low, and the prices are easy to manipulate, which could mean that you could buy the shares, but might not be able to sell them later, therefore, penny stocks are the least favorable options of all.

And if you're thinking that you would invest a little in all small companies hoping that at least one of them would make a 10-20 fold return and make a profit, let me tell you that there are more than 700 such stocks in the stock market, or to be precise, at the time of writing this book, there are 762 stocks with share price less than 10 INR. So, it's not possible to guess which stock would perform well.

SMALL-CAP STOCKS:

This option is best for the ones who wish to make it big and have the heart to take a risk. I believe this category is where the real investing game begins. These stocks belong to companies which have a relatively low market capitalization, but they possess an untapped potential for multifold growth. Small-cap stocks are often overlooked by common investors. This makes them an interesting option for those who don't mind trying something different or less popular.

Penny stocks and small-cap stocks are different in many ways. Small-cap stocks are more stable and have a better chance of growing. These companies usually have a good business base, creative products or services, and space to grow in their markets. They can be a bit risky, but they often have better cash flow, a longer history, and a better chance of success in the long run than penny stocks.

There are stocks in the small-cap sector whose share

prices could be anything, but their market cap is usually less than INR 5000 crores. Companies with a market cap of 1-2 crores also fit the definition of small-cap stocks. However, if you want high returns and are willing to take a bit of a high risk, you can consider small-cap stocks, but invest in companies that have at least a market cap of 1000 crores. Along with this, look for companies whose sales and profits are growing at a compound annual growth rate (CAGR) of 15%, and have low debt or liabilities.

Let's consider another company named Jyoti Resins and Adhesives Ltd., which makes various types of wood adhesives under the brand name Euro 7000. Its sales have grown at a Compound Annual Growth Rate (CAGR) of 37% in the last five years, and its profit has grown at a CAGR of 113% in the last five years. In 2018, it made a profit of just 1 crore, but by 2023, its profit increased to 46 crores. Hence, its share price was at INR 23 on June 4, 2018, and on May 30, 2023, it rose to 1425 INR, as shown below.

Compounded Sales Growth	
10 Years:	38%
5 Years:	37%
3 Years:	53%
TTM:	44%

Compounded Profit Growth	
10 Years:	56%
5 Years:	113%
3 Years:	81%
TTM:	153%

Stock Price CAGR	
10 Years:	85%
5 Years:	120%
3 Years:	211%
1 Year:	91%

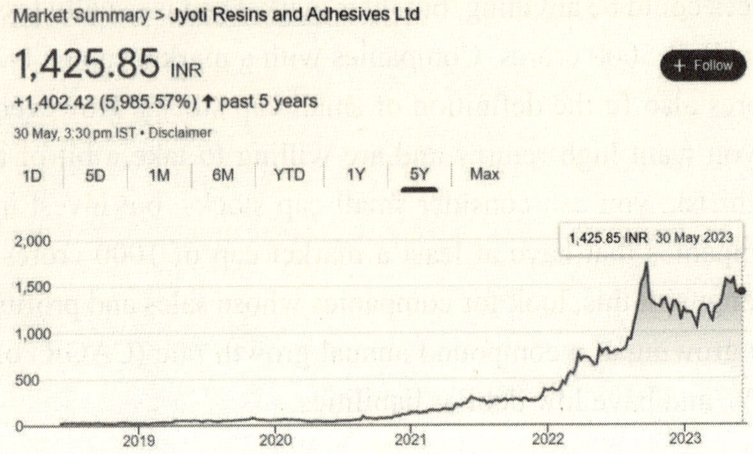

This means that the stock has multiplied the investors' money more than 60 times in five years. In other words, anyone who would've invested INR 1 lakh in this stock five years ago would now have more than INR 60 lakh. The clear reason for this is the increase in its sales and profit.

Similarly, there is another stock named Tanla Platforms Ltd., which is an IT sector company. Its sales have increased at a CAGR of 33% and profit at 93% in the last five years. In 2018, it made a profit of just 19 crores, but by 2023, its profit increased to 448 crores. This led to an increase in its share price, which was INR 30 on June 22, 2018, and it rose to INR 2061 by June 14, 2022. Currently, on May 30, 2023, it's trading at 763 INR. So, if we compare it with the all-time high, this stock has yielded a return of 68 times, and even if we compare it with the present, it has yielded a return of 25 times.

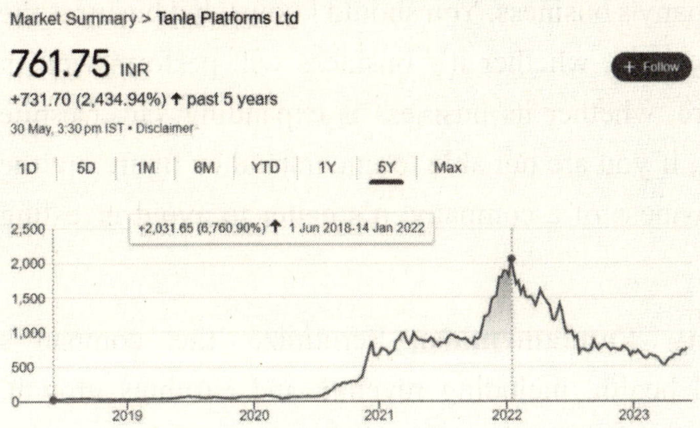

So, if you're looking for a stock that can provide multibagger returns, i.e., multiply your money many times, you can invest in such small-cap stocks that are consistently increasing their sales and profits, while avoiding penny stocks. But keep in mind, with the pursuit of high returns comes increased risk. While such stocks have the potential for high profits, they can also lead to significant losses if your research is flawed or incorrect. Let's move to the next section to understand what key factors are to be considered when searching for strong small-cap stocks.

IDENTIFYING GOOD SMALL-CAP STOCKS

To unlock the potential of small-cap stocks, one must master the art of analysis and research. Here are some factors to consider when identifying good small-cap stocks to invest in:

Business Model: First and foremost; you need to understand the company's business. You should know what business the company is in, whether it's business will perform well in the future, whether its business is expanding, etc. Despite research, if you are not able to understand or figure out the exact business of a company, it's better to avoid investing in it.

Company Fundamentals: Scrutinize the company's financial health, including revenue and earnings growth, profitability, debt levels, and cash flow. Look for companies with a track record of consistent performance and a sound business model capable of withstanding market fluctuations. How much is the company's sales growth? What is profit growth? Generally, if a company's sales and profits are growing at a CAGR of more than 15%, it is considered good. For the company to give good returns, it should not have too much debt or liabilities. The debt-to-equity ratio is used to measure debt, and it is better if it is less than 1.

Management Team: Evaluate the leadership and expertise of the company's management team. Strong, capable leaders with a clear vision and a proven ability to execute strategies are essential for long-term success. Keep in mind, a company doesn't function on its own; it is run by promoters and management teams. The management is essentially the driving force of the company, and only if they have a solid background and business experience can they successfully steer the company towards progress. Evaluating the quality and experience of the management team is as crucial in assessing a company as any other aspect.

Market Opportunity: Assess the industry and market trends in which the company operates. Identify growth potential, competitive landscape, and any regulatory or technological factors that may impact the company's growth prospects. Companies operating in emerging industries or niche markets may hold significant potential for future expansion.

Valuation: Consider the stock's valuation relative to its growth potential. A reasonably priced small-cap stock with room for appreciation can present an attractive investment opportunity. Even if you buy good stocks at expensive prices, there's a higher chance that you will incur losses. For example, I mentioned Tanla Platforms earlier, whose share price rose from 30 rupees to 2061 rupees. Let's suppose you had bought that stock at INR 2061, now the share price has fallen to INR 763, meaning in this situation, you would have incurred a significant loss. Therefore, always pay attention to the valuation of the stock. To determine whether a stock is expensive or cheap, the PE ratio is used. Generally, it is believed that if the stock's PE ratio is less than the PE ratio of its industry, then the stock is considered undervalued, i.e., cheap. If the stock's PE ratio is more than its industry PE ratio, then it is considered overvalued, i.e., expensive. Although, this is not a strict rule, and it differs from company to company and as well as industry.

SMALL-CAP STOCKS TRIUMPHS

Let me tell you about a remarkable investor I came to know of: Porinju Veliyath. A common man belonging from Kerala, made a big name in stock market investment. If you're looking to get better at understanding and working in the stock market, there's a lot you can learn from Veliyath's story.

Veliyath came from a simple background, growing up in a small village called Chalakudy near Kochi, Kerala. He started his career in Mumbai, working as a floor trader with Kotak Securities and then as a research analyst with Parag Parikh Securities. In 2002, he moved back to Kochi and started his own company. What's amazing is how he managed to stand out by focusing on companies that others weren't paying attention to.

I often find myself discussing the success stories of Porinju Veliyath among investors and analysts. His portfolio saw explosive growth during the stock market bull run from 2013 to 2018, mostly due to his investments in what came to be known as multi-bagger stocks. These investments brought him huge returns, further solidifying his stature as a savvy investor who can identify hidden gems.

In 2016, he even foresaw the bright future of Reliance Industries with Jio, gaining the attention of many in the investment community. A classic example of his investment prowess is his early investment in Geojit Financial Services, a small-cap company that most others overlooked. Even though this stock wasn't popular initially, Veliyath's belief in its potential paid off when it turned into a multi-bagger, generating massive returns. This wise move is a testament to his ability to see future growth prospects beyond immediate circumstances.

Another notable example is his investment in Shreyas Shipping & Logistics. He bought it for Rs 30 in 2012 and sold it at a staggering Rs 839 in 2015. This investment exhibits the importance of understanding market cycles and knowing when to pull out of investments just at the right time.

Overall, Porinju Veliyath's investment philosophy clearly revolves around identifying lesser-known gems, investing in honest companies with a clear business visibility, and maintaining a diversified portfolio.

FUNDAMENTAL ANALYSIS CHECKLIST

Based on several approaches, experiences and studies, I have created a comprehensive checklist for fundamental analysis of any stock that anyone can follow before they invest in any company:

1. **Company Overview**

   - Understand the business model - What does the company do to make money?
   - What industry and sector does the company belong to?
   - Check the company's geographical markets - Are they local, regional, national, or international?

2. **Financial Health**

   - Analyze financial statements: income statement, balance sheet, and cash flow statement.
   - Liquidity ratios: current ratio, quick ratio.
   - Profitability ratios: Net profit margin, return on assets (ROA), return on equity (ROE), Return on capital employed (ROCE).
   - Debt ratios: debt to equity ratio, interest coverage ratio.
   - Efficiency ratios: inventory turnover, accounts receivable turnover.
   - Valuation ratios: price to earnings (P/E) ratio, price to book (P/B) ratio.
   - Market cap > 1000 crore

3. **Look at key financial ratios and indicators mentioned below.**

   - Debt to Equity ratio < 1
   - Net Profit Margin > 15 %
   - Expansion Capacity

- Geographical expansion capacity
- Pledged Shares < 5%
- 3 yrs Profit growth > 15 %
- 3 yrs Sales Growth > 15 %
- Return on Equity > 15 %
- Return on Capital Employed > 15 %

4. Management and Corporate Governance

- Evaluate the competence and integrity of the management team.
- Evaluate the effectiveness of the Board of Directors.
- Check for any corporate governance issues.

5. Industry Analysis

- Understand the industry dynamics - Is the industry growing, stable, or declining?
- Analyze the competition - Who are the company's main competitors? What are their strengths and weaknesses?
- Evaluate the regulatory environment - Are there new regulations that could impact the industry?

6. Macro-Economic Factors

- Assess the overall economic environment - Are we in an economic upturn or downturn?
- Assess the impact of political, economic, socio-cultural, technological, environmental, and legal (PESTEL) factors on the industry and company.

- Consider the effects of currency fluctuations if the company operates internationally.

7. **Investment Thesis**

   - Develop a clear investment thesis - Why do you think the company is a good or bad investment?

8. **Determine the company's intrinsic value - Is the current market price over or under this value?**

9. **Evaluate the potential risks - What could go wrong with your investment thesis?**

As our enthralling battle between small-cap stocks and penny stocks reaches its heights, the resounding victor emerges — small-cap stocks. As we draw the curtain on this chapter, I hope you now understand the difference between small-cap stocks and penny stocks. As you embark on your investment journey, exercise caution and careful consideration. Seek out those small-cap treasures with robust fundamentals, visionary leadership, and promising growth prospects.

CHAPTER 5

MID-CAP AND LARGE-CAP STOCKS

"The most popular investing products are the worst ones for investors."

- Robert Rolih

The Indian stock market is undoubtedly a dynamic, ever-evolving entity with a various option for investment opportunities. More often than not, it is large cap stocks that catch people's eye, mostly because we hear about them or use them in our everyday lives. But there is another category of stocks known as mid-cap stocks that prove to be fertile hunting ground for those investors looking for high growth potential. Let's see what mid-cap stocks are about.

Mid-cap stocks in India, basically represent companies whose market capitalization falls between INR 5000 crores and INR 20,000 crores. These businesses have established a foothold in the market but are still in the growth phase of their business cycle. They offer a blend of stability and growth potential, making them an intriguing proposition for investors. There are several reasons why mid-cap stocks can be particularly attractive in the Indian market. The foremost reason for this is how many mid-cap companies operate in niche sectors or emerging industries that are underrepresented among large-caps. This includes sectors such as specialized chemicals, renewable energy, and online retail, which are currently experiencing rapid growth in India.

Another noteworthy aspect of Indian mid-cap stocks is the potential for significant returns. Many of today's large-cap giants in India, such as Infosys or HDFC Bank, were once mid-cap stocks. The investors who recognized their potential and invested in these companies early have seen substantial capital appreciation. Despite their potential, it's crucial to acknowledge that for every success story, there are several mid-cap stocks that failed to live up to their promise. I cannot emphasize enough how investing in mid-caps necessitates a thorough understanding of the business, its growth prospects, competitive environment, and management quality. One of the defining features of mid-cap stocks is their volatility. Mid-cap stocks in India can be more sensitive to economic shifts and market sentiment than large-cap stocks, leading to larger price swings. This can present buying opportunities during downturns, but it also increases the potential for losses.

Most people keep a keen eye on media and their coverage on companies that they have invested in, but small cap and mid-cap companies often lack the level of analyst coverage and media attention enjoyed by large-cap companies. As a result, investors need to be willing and able to perform their research and due diligence. But investors need to understand that this very lack of media coverage is exactly what they need, because such undervalued opportunities are hiding in plain sight.

Media coverage often leads to sudden price changes, as it can create hype or fear among investors. Small and mid-cap stocks often have lower trading volumes, so their prices can be more susceptible to dramatic fluctuations in response to news coverage. Moreover, media coverage generally focuses on recent events or short-term prospects, which can be distracting from a company's long-term fundamentals and potentially lead to mispricing. Investors might make hasty decisions based on the latest news rather than the company's long-term growth potential.

I have been following media for years now. Media outlets can sometimes misinterpret or oversimplify complex business matters, leading to misunderstandings among investors. Incorrect or misleading information can harm a company's reputation and stock price which may lead to investors selling off the shares at early stages.

Any sudden and Intense media coverage can attract speculative traders who are more interested in short-term price movements than the company's underlying fundamentals. This can increase price volatility and make the stock's performance more unpredictable. Undoubtedly, media coverage leads to more challenges than easement. If a company is constantly in the media spotlight, management may need to spend more time addressing media concerns, potentially diverting their attention from core business operations. Moreover, high media coverage can create inflated expectations. If a company fails to meet these expectations, even slightly, it can result in a harsh sell-off by disappointed investors. So, if you have eyes on a stock that is not in media coverage, don’t worry, it's better to do your fundamental analysis as mentioned in previous chapter and move along the lines.

Let's consider Varun Beverages as an example of a mid-cap stock. This company is the franchise holder for PepsiCo, and it manufactures and sells all of PepsiCo's brands such as Pepsi, Pepsi Black, Mountain Dew, Sting, Seven-Up, Mirinda Orange, Tropicana Slice, Tropicana Juices, Seven-Up Nimbooz, and more in India. Furthermore, it also operates the PepsiCo franchise in Nepal, Sri Lanka, Morocco, Zambia, and Zimbabwe, showing its successful business operations.

In 2018, Varun Beverages had a market capitalization of approximately 14,000 crores, categorizing it as a mid-cap stock. Its sales growth was impressive, showing a 27% increase in 2018 and a 39% increase in 2019. Despite a minor slowdown in 2020 due to the COVID-19 pandemic, its sales bounced back with a 36% increase in 2021 and a remarkable 49% increase in 2022. Over the past five years, the company's sales have grown at a compound annual growth rate (CAGR) of 27%, and its profit has soared by 49%.

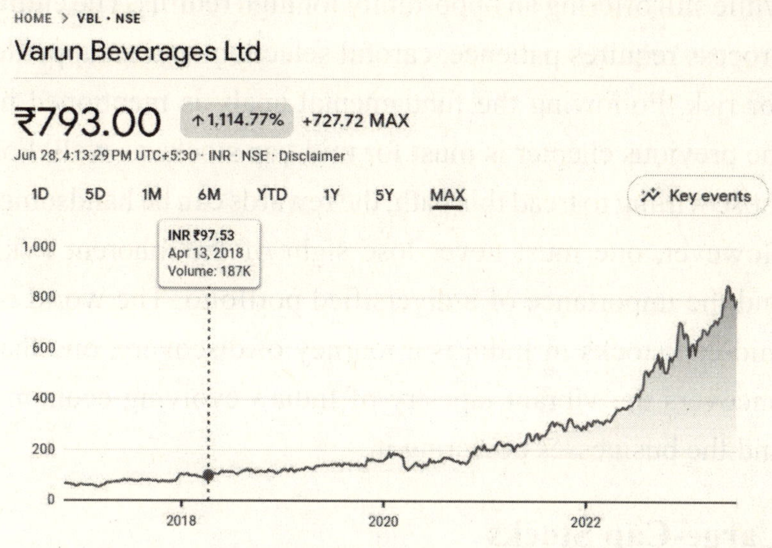

These robust financials significantly impacted its share price. While a share of Varun Beverages was priced at Rs 97 in 2018, it's currently trading around Rs 800. This has led to a surge in its market capitalization, reaching nearly 1 lakh crores, transitioning the company from a mid-cap to a large-cap stock. Over five years, it has managed to amplify investors' capital by eight times, primarily due to its rapid and consistent growth in sales and profit.

Overall, we can say, investing in mid-cap stocks in India, like anywhere else, is a delicate balancing act. On the one hand, they offer substantial growth potential that large-caps may not provide. On the other hand, they carry higher risks. The key to navigating this landscape successfully is diversification. A well-balanced portfolio, containing a mix of large, mid, and small-cap stocks, can help mitigate risk while still offering an opportunity for high returns. The entire process requires patience, careful selection, and an appetite for risk. Following the fundamental analysis mentioned in the previous chapter is must for mid-cap stocks as well. For those willing to tread this path, the rewards can be handsome. However, one must never lose sight of the inherent risks and the importance of a diversified portfolio. The world of mid-cap stocks in India is a journey of discovery, one that uncovers the vibrant tapestry of India's evolving economy and the businesses powering it.

Large-Cap Stocks

The Indian stock market is a home to over 5,000 publicly traded companies, including a diverse mix of stocks spanning across market capitalizations. While mid-cap and small-cap stocks often attract investors seeking high-growth opportunities, large-cap stocks play a critical role in shaping a robust and well-diversified investment portfolio. In this section, I'll shed light on the dynamics of large-cap stocks in India.

Large-cap companies in India typically have a market capitalization of INR 20,000 crores or above. This segment includes some of India's most esteemed and recognized corporations such as Reliance Industries, Tata Consultancy Services, and Hindustan Unilever. With a significant footprint in their respective industries and an established market presence, these companies act as the backbone of the

Indian economy. This is why large-cap stocks in India are known for their stability and resilience, they have a proven track record of weathering economic downturns and market volatility. Furthermore, they are typically better capitalized and have more diversified revenue streams compared to smaller companies. This allows them to withstand economic shocks and maintain a steady course, providing investors with a sense of security.

It is essential to remember that while large-cap stocks offer stability and dividends, they may not provide the same degree of explosive growth potential that some mid-cap or small-cap stocks might offer. Large-cap stocks are often mature businesses operating in saturated markets, and thus, their growth rates may be slower in comparison.

Another facet of investing in large-cap stocks in India is the level of transparency and corporate governance. As these companies are closely followed by analysts and regulatory bodies, they generally maintain high standards of corporate governance and financial disclosure. This can significantly reduce the risk of unpleasant surprises that can sometimes occur with smaller, less-followed companies. Despite the many benefits, investing in large-cap stocks is not without risks, since they are not entirely immune to market volatility. Factors such as changes in government policies, fluctuations in global commodity prices, or shifts in economic trends can impact their performance. Therefore, thorough research and continual monitoring are essential when investing in large-cap stocks.

Keep in mind that the market capitalization of the company should exceed 20,000 crores to be categorized as large-cap stock. If the company's sales and profit growth is over 10%, that's acceptable. Given the already significant size of such a company, increasing sales and profits becomes challenging. However, performance metrics such as Return on Equity (ROE) and Return on Capital Employed (ROCE) should ideally be above 15%. The company's debt-to-equity ratio should be less than 1. While the promoters' shareholding percentage isn't necessarily a crucial factor, investments from Foreign Institutional Investors (FIIs) and Domestic Institutional Investors (DIIs) are positive signs. Additionally, if promoters, DIIs, or FIIs are incrementally increasing their holdings, it can be considered another positive indicator.

For example, you can look at the chart below, which is for Reliance Industries. In this chart, the green line represents the 50-day Exponential Moving Average (EMA), and the red line represents the 100-day EMA. Since the green line (50 EMA) is above the red line (100 EMA), this indicates that the stock is in a bullish phase, and the share price could potentially increase.

You can see another example below, which is the stock chart for Wipro. Here too, the red line represents the 100-day EMA and the green line represents the 50-day EMA. However, in this case, the red line is above the green line, indicating that the stock is bearish, meaning the price could potentially decrease.

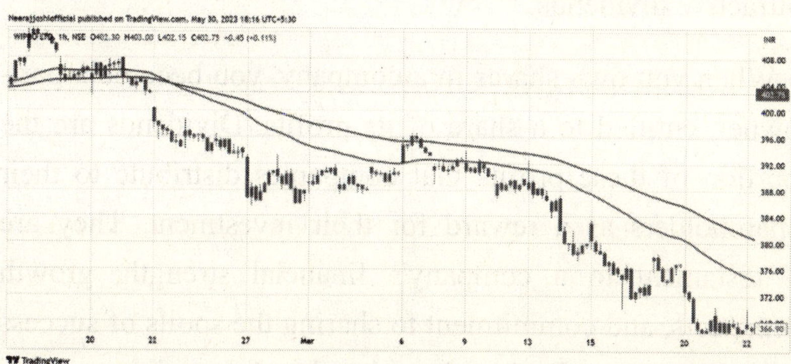

Overall, large-cap stocks in India offer a combination of stability, consistent returns, and income in the form of dividends. They are a critical component of any well-rounded portfolio. While they might not always provide the spectacular short-term returns that some smaller stocks might, their long-term performance and resilience during turbulent times make them a compelling proposition for investors seeking steady growth and lower risk. As always, a diversified approach combining large-cap, mid-cap, and small-cap stocks according to an individual's risk tolerance and investment goals will often yield the best results.

Dividend Stocks

One of the attractive features of many large-cap stocks in India is their tendency to distribute a portion of their earnings to shareholders in the form of dividends. This is particularly appealing to income-oriented investors. Companies like Indian Oil Corporation and Power Grid Corporation of India, among others, have a consistent history of paying attractive dividends.

When you own shares in a company, you become a part-owner, entitled to a share of its profits. Dividends are the portion of these profits that companies distribute to their shareholders as a reward for their investment. They are a testament to a company's financial strength, growth prospects, and commitment to sharing the spoils of success with its owners. Dividend stocks, therefore, offer a unique opportunity to earn a steady stream of passive income, allowing investors to sip on the sweet nectar of financial freedom.

Now, you may wonder, how can one identify good dividend-paying companies? Firstly, pay attention to the company's dividend history. Look for companies that have a consistent track record of paying dividends and even increasing them over time. This demonstrates a commitment to rewarding shareholders and suggests a stable and growing business. Secondly, assess the company's financial health, carry out the fundamental analysis. Look for stocks with strong cash flows, healthy balance sheets, and sustainable payout ratios. These factors contribute to the reliability and longevity of dividends.

A company distributes dividends based on its face value, which typically ranges from 1 to 10 rupees. Suppose a company's share price is 1000 rupees, and its face value is 10 rupees. If the company declares a dividend of 10 rupees per share, it is reported in the news as the company providing a 100% dividend. Hearing the term '100% dividend' tends to make investors happy, but in reality, if you consider the share price, it represents just a 1% dividend yield. Therefore, to accurately assess the dividends a company is offering, you should always consider the dividend yield, not the percentage of the face value that is being paid out as a dividend.

People often claim to be receiving dividends worth INR 1 Lakh. That is only possible if you have invested lakhs of rupees. For instance, HCL currently has a dividend yield of

4.2 %, this implies - if someone has invested INR 25 Lakhs more, then he or she might receive dividends worth a lakh or so.

One of the most common mistakes made by people is investing in companies that are giving out a good dividend amount, but their returns are decreasing with time, meaning; their share prices keep going lower. Such people may receive dividends, but they are bound for a huge loss. Often, announcements by companies to stop giving out dividends lead to negative sentiments and a decrease in their stock price. Therefore, despite being in loss, they take on more debt to keep paying out dividends to their shareholders, but then again, the shareholders remain unaware of this debt and face losses in future when the prices plummet too low.

Reinvesting Dividends:

If you are receiving dividends from a well-established stable company, I suggest you reinvest the dividends. It is a secret sauce that can transform your wealth-building journey. When you reinvest dividends, you use the money received from dividends to buy more shares of the same company, compounding your returns over time. This simple act of reinvestment can have a profound impact on your wealth. As you acquire more shares, your ownership stake in the company grows, leading to larger dividend payments in the future. It's like a snowball rolling downhill, gathering momentum and size as it rolls. Over the long term, the power of reinvested dividends can work wonders, multiplying your initial investment and helping you achieve financial milestones

Currently there are many stock market giants that provide dividends to their stockholders, such as ITC, HCL, Wipro and many more. Check out their list and do the needful analysis before you decide to dip your money into these companies.

CHAPTER 6

STRATEGY FOR MID CAP OR LARGE CAP STOCKS

"Opportunities come infrequently. When it rains gold, put out the bucket, not the thimble."

– Warren Buffett

On 24th January 2023, Hindenburg Research took the world by a storm when it released a report on the Adani Group. The report led to one event after another, like falling dominoes. This report contained some serious allegations against the richest man in India and the 3rd richest in the world. The lengthy report consisted of various names, documents, numbers, etc., intended to prove that the group had been involved in stock manipulation, accounting fraud, and corporate governance lapses.

This report not only stirred the stock market circles but also the political ones. As a direct result of this report, the share price, which was INR 2,166 two weeks prior, had come down to INR 762. To many investors, buying at this time seemed like a death trap; but I saw it as an opportunity. Before buying into it, I carried out thorough research and found that Hindenburg had stated, *"We have Taken a short position in Adani Group Companies through U.S.-traded bonds and non-Indian-traded derivative instruments."* This implied that there were high chances of this report being biased for financial or political purposes.

Overall, the effect of this report on the share prices seemed like a temporary effect. I realized that the share price had plummeted quite low, but eventually, it would rise again. I knew that after I bought the shares, the price could plummet even lower before going up. Because in such cases, the exact bottom cannot be predicted, which reminds me of Vijay Kedia, one of the most eminent investors in the Indian stock market, who often says, "only two people can buy at the bottom and sell at the top. The first one is God, and the other is a liar."

As you can see below, the lowest point reached by the share price of Adani Green was INR 462. At this point, I saw a loss of INR 2.5 lakhs in my portfolio. But fortunately, as I had expected, the price began to rise and I sold my position at INR 848, even though I knew the price would rise further. I had to sell early because of the 5% upper circuit on this stock. Despite everything, I made a profit of INR 1 lakh on my investment of INR 10 lakhs on 20th March.

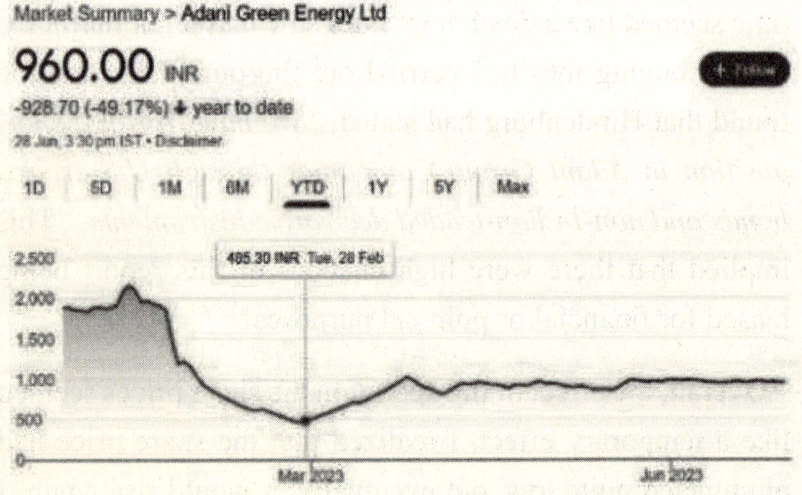

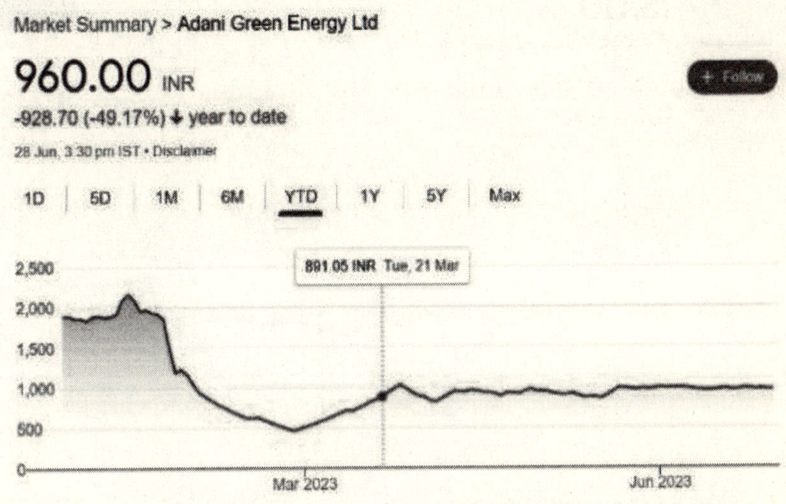

On 21st March 2023, I took the entire amount and invested it in Adani ENT. This is because the share price of Adani ENT had decreased by 60% from its all-time high. On 21st March, at the price of INR 1,824, I bought the shares, investing almost INR 11 lakhs. Thereafter, the price dropped further to INR 1,600. I kept my calm despite the evident loss visible in my portfolio.

Within 2-3 months, the price had begun to rise. In the last 5 days from 22nd May, the price had risen by 21.6%. On 22nd May, the price had increased by 19.5%, and I could see a profit of more than INR 3 lakhs in my portfolio.

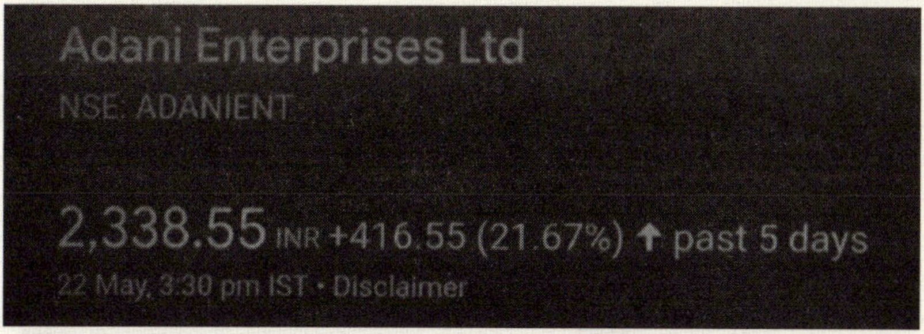

Adani Enterprises Ltd
NSE: ADANIENT

2,338.55 INR +416.55 (21.67%) ↑ past 5 days
22 May, 3:30 pm IST • Disclaimer

Adani Enterprises Ltd
NSE: ADANIENT

2,338.55 INR +382.50 (19.55%) ↑ today
22 May, 3:30 pm IST • Disclaimer

Adani Group is not the only example of such opportunities. Reliance also experienced a sudden dip. The share price of Reliance INDS dropped from INR 1,589 to INR 867 as the Corona pandemic started spreading in India and a lockdown was announced. Five months later, the price touched a high of INR 2,367, as shown below. If someone had bought the shares somewhere before or after the bottom, and sold near the top, they could have made a profit of three times their investment.

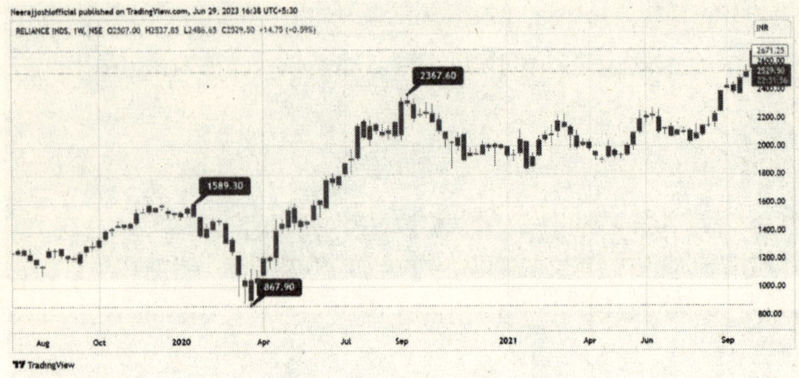

Finolex INDS is another such example. It is a PVC pipes and fittings manufacturing company. The product is essential in the infrastructure sector, on which the government has been focusing. In August 2022, due to a shortage of raw materials and high pricing, the company's profit had significantly decreased, leading to a loss for the first time since its establishment, as you can see below. This decline in profit also had a significant impact on their share price, which dropped from INR 234 down to INR 122.

Quarterly Results

PRODUCT SEGMENTS

Standalone Figures in Rs. Crores / View Consolidated

	Mar 2020	Jun 2020	Sep 2020	Dec 2020	Mar 2021	Jun 2021	Sep 2021	Dec 2021	Mar 2022	Jun 2022	Sep 2022	Dec 2022	Mar 2023
Sales +	769	562	586	1,066	1,249	968	1,083	1,005	1,595	1,190	941	1,125	1,141
Expenses -	665	474	441	720	839	758	783	763	1,330	1,064	1,084	1,033	924
Material Cost %	65%	68%	54%	55%	51%	60%	56%	56%	70%	67%	91%	68%	58%
Employee Cost %	5%	6%	6%	3%	5%	5%	4%	4%	4%	4%	4%	4%	4%
Operating Profit	104	88	145	346	410	210	300	242	265	126	-143	92	217
OPM %	13%	16%	25%	32%	33%	22%	28%	24%	17%	11%	-15%	8%	19%
Other Income +	1	8	32	18	14	15	32	19	401	25	39	28	29
Interest	8	3	1	1	2	5	0	1	8	11	4	5	6
Depreciation	19	19	19	20	20	20	21	21	22	21	22	22	24
Profit before tax	77	74	157	343	402	200	310	239	636	118	-129	92	216
Tax %	28%	26%	24%	25%	26%	27%	24%	26%	22%	15%	27%	22%	27%
Net Profit +	56	55	120	256	297	147	235	178	494	100	-94	72	158
EPS in Rs	0.90	0.89	1.93	4.12	4.79	2.37	3.79	2.87	7.96	1.61	-1.51	1.16	2.55
Raw PDF													

During this decline, I bought almost 6,700 shares on 16th August at the price of INR 145. Right after I bought them, the share price plummeted further to a low of INR 132, and I saw a potential loss of almost INR 82,000. Despite that, I held onto my position, because I knew the potential of the company in the long run, also keeping in mind that this issue with raw material was a temporary one.

Within a few months, the situation improved, and the price of raw material went down. Moreover, foreign investments saw an increase in March 2023, which was certainly a good sign. By May 2023, it showed a profit of more than INR 2.5 lakhs in my portfolio.

Shareholding Pattern

Numbers in percentages

Quarterly Yearly TRADES

	Jun 2020	Sep 2020	Dec 2020	Mar 2021	Jun 2021	Sep 2021	Dec 2021	Mar 2022	Jun 2022	Sep 2022	Dec 2022	Mar 2023
Promoters +	52.47	52.47	52.47	52.47	52.47	52.47	52.47	52.47	52.47	52.47	52.47	52.47
FIIs +	2.35	2.12	2.28	2.73	2.87	4.31	5.74	5.81	5.69	5.59	5.40	5.51
DIIs +	12.93	13.29	12.89	11.84	11.56	10.67	9.84	9.49	9.82	9.60	11.61	12.25
Government +	0.00	0.00	0.00	0.00	0.00	0.00	0.00	0.00	0.00	0.01	0.01	0.01
Public +	31.90	31.77	32.01	32.61	32.76	32.20	31.61	31.88	31.68	31.76	30.15	29.39
Others +	0.35	0.35	0.35	0.35	0.34	0.34	0.34	0.34	0.34	0.34	0.34	0.34

* The classifications might have changed from Sep'2022 onwards.

FINOLEX INDS.	6,700	184.85	145.17	9,72,639.00	12,38,495.00	2,65,856.00 +27.33%	92,460.00 +8.07%

Such opportunities are available in the market, the only requirement is diligent research work. One must keep a keen eye on everything happening in the market. If I want to summarize this strategy, I'd say; go for the stocks of stable companies that have experienced a price correction due to a temporary problem. Now, temporary problems can be anything, from raw material to media hype or even elections. Before you go on to investing, make sure that it is a temporary problem and not a prolonged or permanent one, due to which there is a price decline. Another main aspect of this strategy to keep in mind is 'Timing'. Often, prices fall slightly and people begin investing due to fear of missing out (FOMO), only to end up with huge losses. If I had bought Adani shares when the price went down from INR 4000 to INR 3000, I would've ended up in a great loss. It could've been a possibility that I would've had to sell my position in loss in order to save my capital.

This strategy is riskier than general investing techniques or ways, but less risky than trading. It requires strong research from which you have to objectively deduce the possibilities of further improvement in company's financials and share price. And always remember, patience is the key!

CHAPTER 7

SIP VS LUMPSUM

"It's not whether you're right or wrong that's important, but how much money you make when you're right and how much you lose when you're wrong."

- George Soros

"Should I invest as lumpsum or SIP in stocks?" This is the one of most common question asked by my viewers; hence, I deemed it important to include it in the book. Both the options have their pros and cons, and only applying them in certain ways will ensure their efficient results. So, let's see what happens when two friends decide to take different approaches to the same stock.

Once upon a time, two friends from Delhi decided to invest their money. After much research and analysis of various financial instruments, they finalized two choices - Stock Market or Mutual Funds. After a deeper understanding of both these options, they finally chose to invest in the stock market. Now a question stood before them: whether they should invest in a SIP format or a Lumpsum format? After much discussion, they decided that one should go with the SIP and the other one shall go with the Lumpsum investment. What was the result? We'll find out at the end of the chapter. Before that, let's see what does these two terms mean in the financial world.

SIP refers to Systematic Investment Plan. A SIP is a powerful financial planning tool that helps individuals to build wealth over time. Basically, SIP is a method of investing in stocks or funds, where instead of making a lump-sum investment, you can invest a fixed amount regularly - on a monthly, quarterly or annual basis. Whereas a Lump-sum investment is when you invest a large amount of money all at once instead of spreading it out over time. This strategy can be beneficial because it allows your money to start growing right away, potentially leading to higher returns over the long run.

Now coming back to our example, let's say: Deep invested in form of SIP and Suraj invested in a lumpsum form.

Scenario 1:

In 2014, Deep invested INR 5000 every quarter, for next 3 years in Reliance Industries.

In 2014, Suraj invested INR 60,000 at once in Reliance Industries, and held it for the next 3 years.

In the below image, you can see the price of stock was INR 440 when Suraj had invested a lumpsum amount. After 3 years, since the price rose to INR 536, his investment became worth INR 73,090, which meant that he made a profit of INR 13,090.

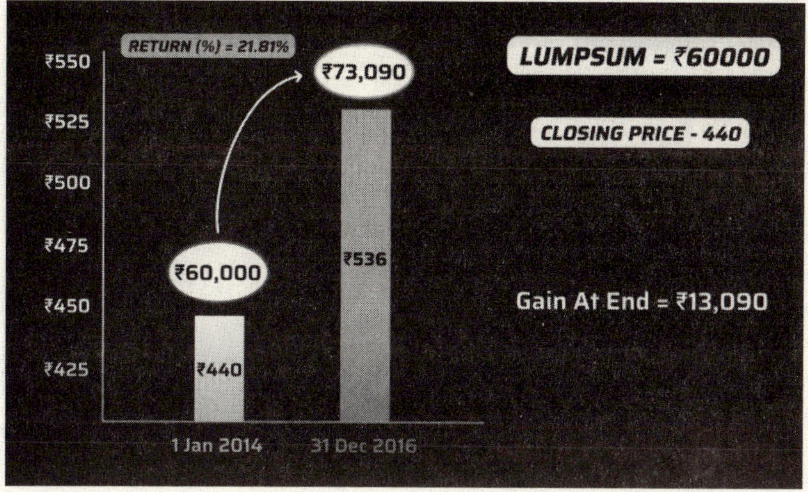

Whereas, in SIP, since the amount was being invested over the period of 3 years, during which the price of the stock kept fluctuating, therefore, the average buy was different every time. If the average price throughout these years is calculated, it would be INR 471. Despite the increasing price of the stock, Deep kept buying stock every quarter. As a result, Suraj made a profit of 21.8%, whereas Deep only made a profit of 13.8%. But could the results be different if the situation was altered?

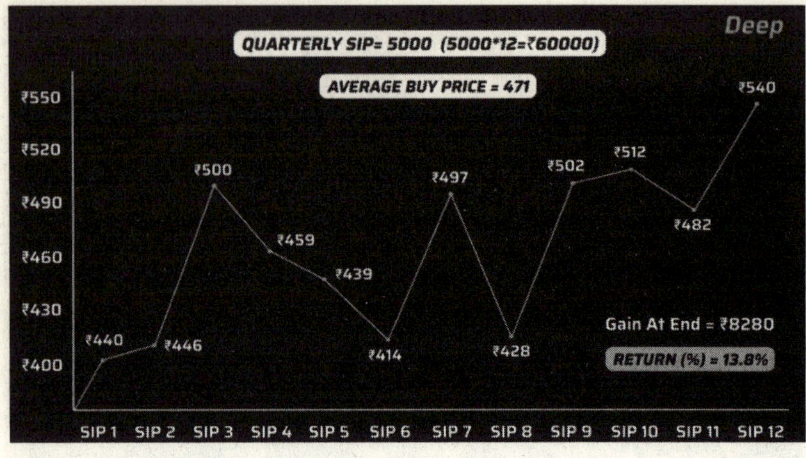

Scenario 2:

In 2015, Deep invested INR 10,000 per month in Tata Motors for next 4 years.

In 2015, Suraj invested INR 4.80 lakh in Tata Motos, and held it for next 4 years.

Conclusion: In the below image we can see, during this time period, Tata Motors did not perform well, due to which Suraj incurred a loss of -64.50% on his investment. Whereas, because of cost averaging in SIP format, Deep only incurred a loss of - 57% on his investment. We can say that investing in SIP format saved Deep from incurring more loss as compared to Suraj.

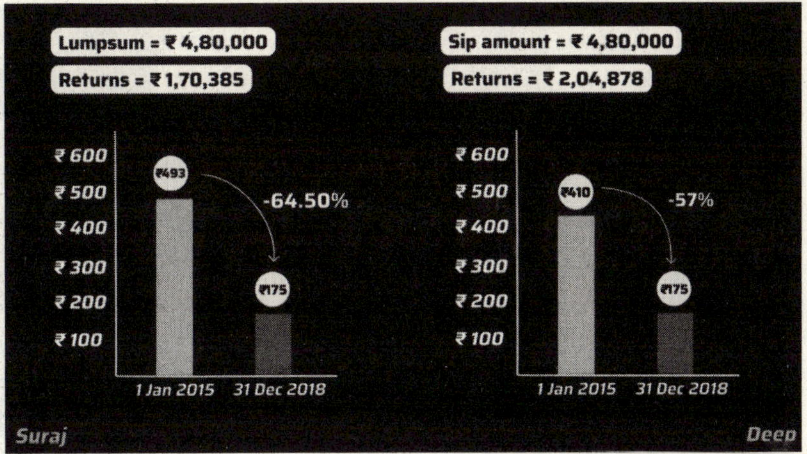

Scenario 3:

In 2015, Deep invested INR 5000 per month but for 8 years in Tata Motors.

In 2015, Suraj invested INR 4.80 Lakhs all at once for next 8 years in Tata Motors.

Conclusion: in the below image we can see, when Suraj invested a lumpsum amount; the price of the share was INR 493. Thereafter, the price kept falling, even hitting the low of INR 67 during Covid pandemic, whereafter it picked up a pace.

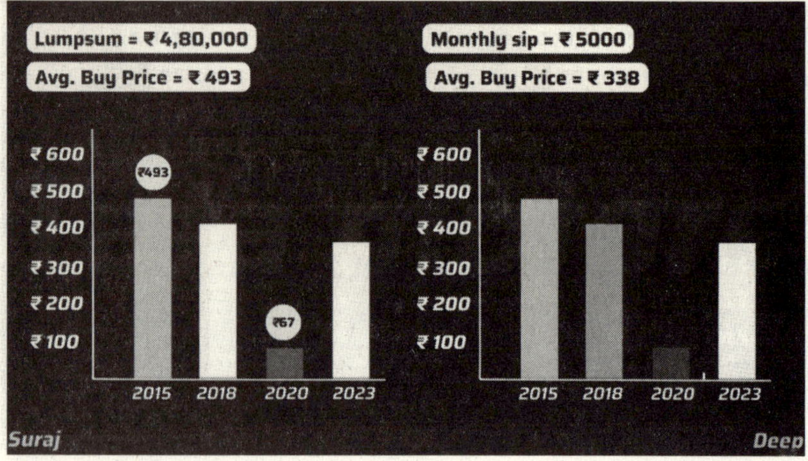

Deep invested every month for 8 years, due to the falling price in these years, the average buy cost turned out to be INR 338. Since Suraj had invested all at once, he couldn't do anything when the price was falling. Whereas, Deep had the advantage of price fall, and he could buy more shares for a lower price.

If we compare the above prices to the current price (while I am writing this book) which is INR 530, we can see who made the most profit. In the below image we can observe, via lumpsum investment Suraj received a profit of only 36,000, which is only 7.5% return on the investment. While in Deep's case, he received a profit of INR 2,72,662 Lakhs, which is 56% return on the investment.

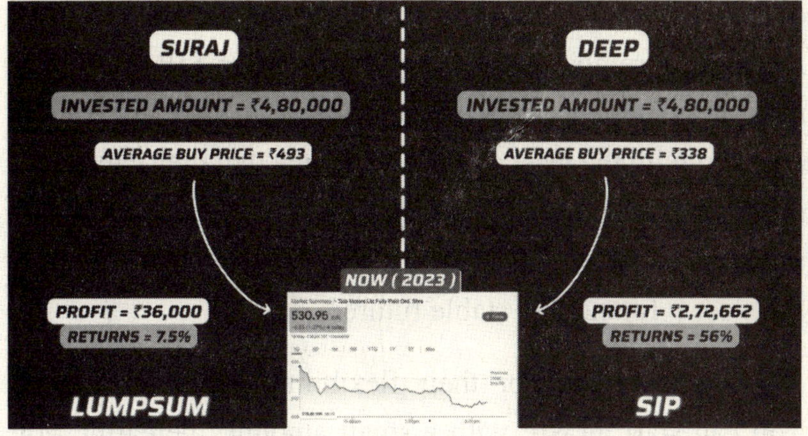

After analyzing all the three scenarios the conclusion is:

- It is better to invest in lumpsum form when the price is relatively low.

- Considering the market volatility, SIP gives you the advantage of cost averaging.

It would be wrong to say that either option is better than the other one. Both these options can have optimal results if utilized efficiently. In order to get a clearer picture, let's see what the advantages and disadvantages of both are.

SIP Advantages and Disadvantages

An essential feature of SIP is rupee cost averaging. By investing a fixed amount at regular intervals, you can buy more units when the prices are low and fewer units when the prices are high. Over time, this reduces the average cost of investing and mitigates the impact of market volatility. Also, the foremost reason why I emphasize SIP is; anyone regardless of their profession or studies can start an SIP. One can start with the least amount of money that they can invest monthly, be it out of their salary or pocket money. Therefore, it provides a good opportunity for students to start investing early for a financially stable future.

SIPs are known for their flexibility and convenience. You can start an SIP with a small amount, thereafter, you can also modify, pause, or stop your SIP at any time, and choose a tenure that aligns with your financial goals. It is a handy tool for achieving long-term financial goals. Whether it's saving for retirement, buying a home, or funding your child's education, investing regularly via SIP can help grow your wealth over time. The power of compounding, where you earn returns on your returns, plays a significant role in wealth creation, particularly if you start investing at an early age. Moreover, it also helps in avoiding impulsive investment decisions based on market fluctuations or emotional biases. SIP fosters discipline, harnesses the power of compounding, and allows the investors to navigate the ups and downs of the market with poise.

However, it's crucial to remember that SIPs are not a guarantee of high returns. The performance of your SIP will depend on the performance of the mutual fund or stock you choose. One of the greatest disadvantages of SIP is cost averaging. As shown in the above example, the price of share kept rising, and deep kept investing and buying the shares, which lead to a higher average buy price, which impacted the profit on the investment.

The below calculation shows the result of an SIP with INR 5000 investment per month for next 10 years with 10% returns.

Projection for 10 years

Future investment value	Initial balance
₹10,24,224.89	₹0.00
Wealth gain	**Additional deposits**
₹4,24,224.89	₹6,00,000.00
	Percentage (yearly)
	10%

the Calculator site

Let's suppose your salary increases 20 percent each year, due to which you also decide to increase your monthly investment by 10%. The below calculation shows how great of an impact a small change can make.

Projection for 10 years

Future investment value ₹15,10,340.20	Initial balance ₹0.00
Wealth gain ₹5,54,094.40	Additional deposits ₹9,56,245.80
	Percentage (yearly) 10%

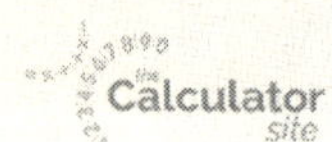

Lumpsum Advantages and Disadvantages:

Lumpsum has the potential for higher returns with time. When you invest a large sum all at once, you expose all of your money to the potential for growth immediately. Over a long-term period, historically, markets tend to rise, and hence lump-sum investing has often led to higher returns. Lump-sum investing simplifies the investment process by eliminating the need for regular contributions. Once you make your initial investment, there's no need to continually monitor and make decisions about when and how much to invest. With lump-sum investing, your money has more time to grow, and you reap the benefits of compounding for a longer period, as compared to SIP system.

Nonetheless, Lump-sum certainly has an element of risk, or you could say 'regret', because it exposes you to the risk of poor timing. If the market declines shortly after you invest, you could see a substantial decrease in the value of your investment, as shown in the example above. Investing all at once limits your opportunities for diversification, if you invest everything into one place at one time. Spreading your investments across different assets (diversification) — can help manage risk and even gain better returns. If you invest a large sum all at once, the impact of market fluctuations can be more emotionally challenging. Seeing a large decline in investment in value can lead to panic and poor decision-making.

Strategies for Success:

To truly savor the rewards of SIP or Lumpsum investments, it's important to adopt some key strategies. Firstly, choose the right investment vehicle. Both of these options can be initiated in various financial instruments, such as mutual funds, stocks, or even gold. Consider your financial goals, risk appetite, and investment horizon to select the most suitable option. Secondly, be consistent with your contributions if it's an SIP. Set a comfortable investment amount that you can commit to on a regular basis. Consistency is the key to reaping the rewards of SIP investments. And lastly, embrace the long-term perspective when it comes to both options. These options are designed for gradual wealth creation, so don't get swayed by short-term market fluctuations. Savor the journey and let compounding work its magic over time.

CHAPTER 8

MUTUAL FUNDS AND ITS TYPES

"If you have the stomach for stocks, but neither the time nor the inclination to do the homework, invest in equity mutual funds."

- Peter Lynch

Mutual funds are an important aspect of stock market, I believe, because they provide a viable investment option for individuals who may not have the time, knowledge, or resources to manage their own diverse portfolio of individual stocks. It is basically a type of investment strategy where many people pool their money together to buy different types of investments like stocks, bonds, and other assets. These funds are managed by financial professionals, which allows individual investors to access well-managed and diversified portfolios that would be otherwise difficult to handle on their own. Each fund follows a specific investment strategy, focusing on certain types of investments, industries, or risk levels. The profits made from these investments, such as dividends from stocks or interest from bonds, are distributed among the investors based on the number of shares they own in the fund. Mutual funds are popular because they provide easy access, professional management, and the benefits of diversification. However, it's important to consider the risks and fees associated with mutual funds before investing.

One major advantage of mutual funds is diversification. By investing in a single mutual fund, you can own a wide range of securities from many different companies. This helps reduce the impact of poor performance from any one investment. For example, if a fund holds 100 stocks and one of them does poorly, it will only have a small effect on the overall portfolio because that stock represents a small portion of the total holdings. This spreading of risk is a key benefit of mutual funds.

In addition, mutual funds offer the advantage of professional management. Fund managers and their teams have extensive experience and resources to analyze market trends, economic data, and individual investments. They use this knowledge to make informed decisions on when to buy or sell securities for the fund. This expertise, which individual investors may not have access to, can potentially lead to better investment returns and lower risk.

Mutual funds also provide accessibility and convenience. They usually have low minimum investment requirements, allowing small investors to create diversified portfolios. For example, an individual may not have enough money to buy various stocks and bonds individually, but they can invest in a mutual fund that holds those securities. Additionally, mutual fund investors can rely on professional fund managers to handle investment decisions, relieving them from the need to select and manage individual investments.

Moreover, there is a wide range of mutual funds available to cater to different investor needs and risk tolerances. Whether someone prefers lower risk or is willing to take on more risk, seeks regular income or long-term growth, or has a specific investment timeframe, there is likely a mutual fund that suits their requirements. From funds focused on stocks to those focused on bonds, from funds targeting specific sectors to those designed for particular target dates, the variety of mutual fund options allows investors to tailor their portfolios to meet their specific financial goals and risk tolerance.

Now, the question is - how can you choose the best mutual funds for you to invest in? And where can you invest in them? Every day AMCs bring new funds to the market to attract us, and every high rated mutual fund is not made according to our goal, risk, and investment period, so, we have to find funds that pass all our criteria. Since, there are three types of mutual funds - equity funds, debt funds, and hybrid funds, before choosing equity funds, let's understand the other two as well.

Debt funds are a type of mutual fund that invest in fixed-income securities like bonds and treasury bills. They are considered safer than equity funds because they provide a steady income to investors, making them a preferred choice for conservative investors seeking a low-risk profile. The primary sources of income for debt fund investors are interest earnings and capital gains or losses from the sale of these securities. The main risk in debt funds is very low since your money is invested in government bonds or corporate bonds where returns are fixed. But where the risk is low, the return is low as well. On the other hand, hybrid funds are a mix of equity funds and debt funds, and that's why they are also known as mixed asset funds. There are many types of hybrid funds where the percentage of equity and debt varies. For example, aggressive hybrid funds, conservative hybrid funds, balanced hybrid funds. But right now, our main focus is on equity funds.

Equity funds comprise of 5 types, let's compare them all and see where you can invest.

6 types:

- Index Funds (Most Popular)
- Large Cap Funds
- Mid Cap Funds
- Small Cap Funds
- Multi Cap Fund
- Flexi Cap Funds

Index Funds are investments that put your money into different groups of stocks. These groups are called indices, like Nifty50, Sensex, Nifty Bank, and Nifty Pharma. When you invest in an index fund, your money is divided and invested in the same way as the companies in the index. As the index grows, your investment also grows. Index funds are called passive funds because they don't need a fund manager to make regular changes. On the other hand, active funds are managed by fund managers who make changes based on what they think is best.

Large-cap funds are a type of investment that focuses on big and well-established companies. These funds invest your money in stocks of large companies that are considered leaders in their industries. The goal of large-cap funds is to provide stability and long-term growth. They are generally seen as less risky compared to funds that invest in smaller or riskier companies.

In **mid-cap funds**, the company that manages the funds invests your money in medium-sized companies. These are companies that are not too big or too small, but in the middle. Specifically, they invest in companies that rank between 101 and 250. So, if you invest in a mid-cap fund, your money will go towards these types of companies.

Small-cap funds are a type of investment that focuses on smaller companies. These funds invest your money in stocks of companies that are considered small in size. These companies typically have a smaller market capitalization and are still in their early stages of growth.

In **Multi-cap funds,** your money is invested in companies of all sizes: large, mid-sized, and small. The idea is to benefit from the different opportunities provided by each category. However, there is a rule that fund managers must follow. It states that a minimum of 25% of the money should be invested in each category. This rule is in place to ensure that fund houses distribute the investments across different company sizes.

Flexi-cap funds are highly favored by investors because they offer more flexibility. Unlike multi-cap funds, there are no strict rules or restrictions for fund managers in allocating your money across different company sizes. They can freely choose the percentage of investment in large, mid-sized, and small companies based on their market predictions. For example, if the fund manager believes that mid-sized companies will perform better, they can invest all of the money in that category, without the obligation to invest a specific portion in each category. This flexibility allows fund managers to make decisions based on their insights and expectations for better returns.

Now the question is, which type of fund is right for you? To understand this, there are two things that you need to comprehend:

Investment horizon	Years	Risk appetite
• Short Term • Mid Term, • Long Term	• 1 to 3 years • 3 to 5 years • More than 5 years	If we talk about risk, you will always encounter some risk in equity as compared to other investments. Some carry higher risks while others have lower risks. You can choose according to your comfort and risk tolerance.

Now based on these two factors, we can analyze funds suitable for us.

Types of Equity Funds	Time Horizon	Risk Appetite
1. Large Cap Funds	• **Long term** (more than 5 years) - Best • **Mid Term** (3 to 5 years) - Best • **Short Term** (less than 3 years) - Not recommended	**High Risk:** If you can take higher risk, then this is not favorable for you, because here, your money is invested in all well-established companies where volatility is very low. Therefore, you cannot get the expected return according to your risk. **Low Risk:** This Fund is favorable for those who have a Low-risk capacity, who want to take less risk and want good returns with low risk.
2. Mid Cap Funds	• **Long term** (more than 5 years) - Best • **Mid Term** (3 to 5 years) - Average	**High Risk:** Mostly, mid-cap companies are also well established, but they are still in the growing phase, which

	• **Short Term** (less than 3 years)- Not recommended	makes them riskier than large-cap companies. If one has a high-risk capacity, then they can invest in mid-cap funds. **Low Risk:** This is not suitable for those with a low-risk appetite.
3. Small Cap Funds	• **Long term** (more than 5 years) - Best • **Mid Term** (3 to 5 years) - Not recommended. • **Short Term** (less than 3 years) - Not recommended	Very High Risk - If you are investing for the long term and your risk appetite is high, then you can also consider small cap funds. Here, you will get higher returns than all other funds, but at the same time, the risk is also the highest. Low Risk - This is not favorable for people with a Low-risk appetite.

4. Multi-Cap Funds	• **Long term** (more than 5 years) - Best • **Mid Term** (3 to 5 years)- Not recommended. • **Short Term** (less than 3 years) - Not recommended	**High Risk -** Your money is invested in all three types of companies here, which reduces the risk compared to small cap funds, nonetheless, you get to see high returns. To invest in this option, your risk appetite should be high. **Low Risk -** Not Favorable for investors with a low-risk capacity.

I don't recommend multi-cap funds for several reasons. As I mentioned earlier, there is a requirement set by SEBI (Securities and Exchange Board of India) that mandates fund managers to invest at least 25% in each category. This restriction limits the flexibility of the fund and prevents the fund manager from fully utilizing their skills.

However, if you still want to invest in funds that cover large, mid-sized, and small companies without such limitations, where the fund manager has the freedom to make investment decisions based on their expertise, then flexi-cap funds are the best choice. In flexi-cap funds, there are no fixed percentages to follow. This means that if the fund manager believes a particular mid-cap company will perform well, they can make changes accordingly, without being bound by any specific requirements. This flexibility allows you to take advantage of every opportunity in the market.

1. Flexi Cap Fund	• **Long term** (more than 5 years) - Best • **Mid Term** (3 to 5 years) - Not recommended. • **Short Term** (less than 3 years) - Not recommended	**High Risk** - Flexi Cap funds can generate high returns as the fund manager allocates the fund based on their experience and skills, which can potentially lead to significantly high returns. However, because the allocation is often made to high-opportunity companies, the risk associated can also be quite high. So, if you have a high- risk appetite, this should certainly be in your portfolio.

2. Index Fund	• **Long term** (more than 5 years) - Best • **Mid Term** (3 to 5 years)- Average. • **Short Term** (less than 3 years) - Not recommended	Since Index Funds only invest in indices like Nifty50 and Sensex, the risk is higher in the short term. But if your time horizon is long term period, an index fund could be the best option for you. Since it's a passive fund, the expense ratio is also very low. Even if you have a high-risk capacity, you should have an index fund in your portfolio, which can also act as a hedge for you. Let's brainstorm; do you think the Nifty will fall from its current price INR 19,000 to 12000 after 5 years? No, right? In the long run, the index of a developing country only increases. Hence, it's a good option for everyone.

If I were to summarize the whole comparison, here are some recommendations based on your investment goals and risk capacity. If you have a high-risk capacity and want to invest for the long term, Small Cap and Flexi Cap Funds can be good options. They have the potential to provide higher returns compared to the risk involved. On the other hand, if you have a low-risk capacity but still want to invest for the long term, Index funds are a suitable choice. They offer a balanced approach with relatively lower risk.

For investors with a mid-term investment horizon of around 3 to 5 years and a high-risk capacity, a combination of Index funds and Mid Cap Funds can be considered. These funds have the potential for growth, but they also come with a higher level of risk due to market volatility.

However, it's important to note that equity funds, including these recommended options, are not suitable for short-term investments. They can be highly volatile and carry a higher risk factor, making them less ideal for short-term goals. Therefore, if you want to invest in mutual funds, it is always recommended to create a long-time horizon and have a clear understanding of your risk capacity. This allows for a more strategic and informed approach to investment, minimizing the potential risks associated with short-term volatility.

Now that you understand which fund type aligns with your investment period and risk capacity, let's focus on choosing the best mutual fund among the options available. To make an informed decision, you need to consider four key factors. The first factor is the Expense Ratio. Since mutual funds are managed by professionals, they charge a certain percentage for their expertise, known as the expense ratio. It typically ranges from 0.1% to 2.25%. For example, if you invest 1000 rupees and the expense ratio is 1%, you will pay 10 rupees as fees, and the remaining 990 rupees would be invested. Generally, an expense ratio below 1.5% is considered good.

The second factor to consider is the available plans within the mutual fund, which are generally of two types.

Direct plan	Regular plan
Third Party - No, here your money is directly invested in mutual funds.	**Third Party** - Yes (Advisor / Brokers / Distributor) - Regular plans are those which you buy through an advisor, broker, or distributor.
Expense Ratio - Low, because you're investing directly, you don't have to pay any commission to an advisor or distributor, which reduces your expense ratio.	**Expense Ratio** - High, Here AMC assumes that you have purchased these plans through an advisor or a distributor, so their commission also gets added to your expense ratio.
Returns - High (Due to low expense ratio your overall return becomes high.)	**Returns - Low** (High expense ratio affects your returns.)

I always recommend choosing the direct funds plan as it helps keep your expense ratio low and potentially increases your returns. In the direct plan, you invest directly with the mutual fund company, bypassing any intermediaries. This eliminates the need to pay commission or distribution fees to intermediaries like brokers or advisors.

DRAWBACKS

While mutual funds offer many benefits, but they also come with certain disadvantages that investors need to be aware of. One of the primary drawbacks relates to costs. Mutual funds incur various fees and expenses, including management fees, administrative costs, and possibly sales charges, all of which can erode returns over time. For instance, a fund with a 2% annual expense ratio effectively deducts 2% of the fund's total assets each year to cover these costs, regardless of whether the fund generates positive returns. Over the long term, these expenses can significantly impact an investor's net returns.

Another disadvantage stems from the lack of control that investors have over the individual securities held within a mutual fund. Since the portfolio is managed by a fund manager, investors cannot dictate which specific securities to buy or sell. They must trust the fund manager's decisions, even if they disagree with them. For instance, even if an investor might have ethical concerns with certain industries or companies, they won't be able to prevent a mutual fund from investing in these entities.

Investing in mutual funds also carries the potential for losses. Just as mutual funds can provide substantial gains when the market performs well, they can also lead to significant losses when the market performs poorly. The value of a mutual fund can fluctuate based on the performance of the securities within its portfolio, meaning investors may lose some or all of the money they've invested. For example, during periods of market volatility, the value of mutual fund shares can decrease rapidly and significantly.

Lastly, some types of mutual funds come with liquidity constraints. Certain funds, like fixed maturity plans or closed-end funds, have a stipulated lock-in period during which investors cannot sell their units. This lack of liquidity can be a disadvantage if an investor needs to access their money during the lock-in period. In such cases, exit loads or penalties may apply, further eating into the investor's returns.

Given these disadvantages, it's critical for potential investors to thoroughly research any mutual fund they're considering, understand all associated costs and risks. Here's a detailed checklist to help you navigate through this process:

Investment Objective: The first step is to clarify your financial goals. Are you investing for retirement, a down payment on a house, your child's education, or some other goal? The time frame and importance of these goals will influence the type of mutual fund you should consider.

Risk Tolerance: Understanding your ability to withstand losses or volatility in your investment portfolio is crucial. If a potential loss of investment would severely impact your financial situation or peace of mind, you might want to consider less risky funds, like those focused on bonds or money market securities.

Asset Class: Decide on the asset class that aligns with your investment objective and risk tolerance. This could include equity funds (higher risk but higher potential returns), bond funds (moderate risk and returns), money market funds (lower risk and lower returns), or a mix.

Fund Performance: Look at how the fund has performed over the long term and in different market conditions relative to its benchmark and peer group. While past performance is not a guarantee of future results, it can provide insight into the fund's relative stability and the fund manager's skills.

Fund Manager: Research the fund manager's experience, investment philosophy, and track record. A fund is likely to perform well if it is managed by an experienced and skilled professional.

Expense Ratio: This is the annual fee that all funds charge their shareholders. It's important to compare expense ratios of similar funds - a lower expense ratio can significantly increase your total returns in the long run.

Fund Size: The size of the fund can impact its ability to efficiently manage its portfolio. Very small funds may not have sufficient assets to diversify effectively, while very large funds may have difficulty achieving high returns due to the sheer volume of assets under management.

Tax Efficiency: Some mutual funds generate a lot of capital gains distributions which could have tax implications. Look for funds that are tax-efficient if you are investing in a non-retirement account.

Turnover Ratio: This reflects how frequently assets within a fund are bought and sold by the managers. A high turnover ratio might indicate a more actively managed fund, which could result in higher transaction costs and tax liabilities.

Consistency: Check whether the fund has consistently stuck to its stated investment strategy. A fund that frequently shifts strategy could be a red flag.

Minimum Investment: Some mutual funds require a minimum investment, which may not be suitable for all investors. Make sure the fund's minimum investment requirement aligns with your budget.

Exit Load: Every mutual fund has a specific time frame or lock-in period. If you withdraw your investment before this period, you may be charged a fee known as an exit load. It's important to pay attention to this factor as many people overlook it. If you invest in equity funds and need to withdraw your investment in the short term due to an emergency, you may incur additional expenses through the exit load. That's why it's advisable to avoid investing money for short periods as you won't benefit from the power of compounding. If you're unsure, it's always wise to choose funds with a very low exit load to minimize any additional charges when withdrawing your investment.

Parag Parikh Flexi Cap Fund, Axis Blue-chip Fund Direct Plan Growth, Tata Digital India Fund Direct Growth, Nippon India Smallcap Fund Direct Growth, are few examples of mutual funds in India. Before making any investment, it's crucial to conduct thorough research and analysis, you may even consider consulting a financial advisor. The checklist above is only to provide a framework for you to completely understand the aspects involved and navigate your decision-making process.

So far, we've talked a lot about mutual funds and their different types, including Index funds. Index funds are a popular choice, and it's worth taking some time to really understand them. But to get what Index funds are all about, you first need to know what 'indices' are.

INDICES

In the Indian financial market, indices play a critical role in marking fund performance and providing a clear picture of the market's overall health. The most well-known index in India is the BSE Sensex (Bombay Stock Exchange Sensitive Index), consisting of 30 of the largest and most actively traded stocks on the BSE. Another major index that you must've heard of is the NSE Nifty (National Stock

Exchange Fifty), which includes 50 diverse stocks from 13 sectors of the economy, which provides a broad market representation. Both the Sensex and Nifty are weighted by Free Float market capitalization, meaning companies with larger Free Float market values have a greater impact on the index's movements. Apart from these, there are also several sector-specific indices like Nifty Bank, Nifty IT, and Nifty Pharma, which track performance within those specific sectors. Also, there are broader indices like the BSE 500 or Nifty 500 that give a more comprehensive view of the market beyond the top 30 or 50 companies. Below is the current status of Nifty 50.

These indices hold a significant importance for multiple reasons. Firstly, they provide a measure of the overall health and trends of the economy and the financial markets. For instance, a rising index may indicate a healthy, growing economy, while a falling index may suggest an economic downturn.

Secondly, indices serve as benchmarks against which individual investments or portfolios can be compared. Mutual fund managers, for instance, often compare their funds' performance to a relevant index to see if they're outperforming or underperforming the market. In turn, this information helps investors assess the skill of the fund manager and decide where to invest their money. This relationship between the two indices is why I have added these two concepts in the same chapter, so you can get a clearer idea.

Indices are also crucial for the creation of index funds and exchange-traded funds (ETFs), which aim to replicate the performance of a specific index. These passive investment strategies have gained popularity due to their low cost and the difficulty many active managers face in outperforming the market.

Further, indices are used in economic research and policy making. Researchers and policymakers use the data to understand economic trends, formulate policies, and gauge the impact of various policy decisions on the markets. These indices also contribute to market transparency by providing a continual flow of information about market movements and pricing of securities, which is crucial for efficient market functioning. Through indices, investors worldwide get insight into the performance of a country's largest and most influential companies, and by extension, its economy. We can say that these indices in India play a vital role in reflecting market sentiment, guiding investment strategies, facilitating economic research, and contributing to overall market transparency.

Now, you must be wondering; on what basis or criteria do these companies make it into the indices? Is it okay to directly invest in these companies without carrying out a fundamental analysis? There are several criteria, on the basis of which companies are judged and included in the index. It's important to note that being included in an index doesn't mean a company will always remain there. Regular reviews are carried out to ensure that the index remains representative of the market. If a company no longer meets the necessary criteria, (for example: a fall in market capitalization) it can be removed from the index, with another company taking its place. The criteria are:

Market Capitalization: The first and most important criterion based on which a stock is included in an Index like Nifty50 or Sensex is its Market Capitalization. If we take the example of Nifty, this index is composed of the Top 50 Companies in the Stock Market. In simple language, Market Capitalization means the total value or size of a company, and the formula to calculate is:

Market cap = Price Of 1 Share x Total number of Outstanding shares

Because Nifty50 includes the top 50 companies in the Stock Market, we know the size of a company by looking at its market cap, which is why the market cap is an important factor. What's important to note here is that the company's entire market capitalization isn't considered; only the Free Float Market Capitalization is taken into account. To calculate the Free Float Market Capitalization, only those shares are included which are freely available to be traded in the market, so the shares of the promoters aren't included. This is why Infosys has a greater weightage in the Nifty50 index than TCS, even though the Market cap of Infosys is half of TCS's. TCS's promoter holds 72.3% of the shares, leaving only 27.7% as TCS's free float holding. In contrast, Infosys's promoter only holds 15.1% of the shares, leaving 84.9% as Infosys's Free Float Market cap. This is why Infosys has a greater weightage than TCS in the Nifty50 index.

So, when we speak of the Nifty50, it consists of the top 50 companies based on Free Float Market cap. The Nifty Next 50 includes the next 50 companies, and the Sensex includes the top 30 companies.

Liquidity: The stocks included in the index should be highly liquid. That means they are regularly traded in large volumes. This ensures that the index remains representative of active companies on the exchange.

Listing History: Some indices require a company to be publicly listed for a certain period before it's eligible for inclusion. This allows the index to include only those companies with a proven track record in the public market.

Industry Representation: Indices often aim to provide a broad representation of the economy, so the companies included should ideally span various industries and sectors.

Financial Health: Some indices may also consider the financial health of the company, ensuring that it has sound financial ratios and a good track record of revenue and earnings over the recent period of time.

Active Status: Companies that are under regulatory scrutiny or have been de-listed from the exchange are typically not included in the index.

INDEX FUNDS

On the basis of the indices, Index funds are created, which can be described as a type of mutual fund that mirrors the portfolio of a specific market index, such as the BSE Sensex or the NSE Nifty50. Such funds are designed to track and match the performance of these indices. Because the fund is passively managed, it doesn't seek to outperform the market but to mirror it. Therefore, the success of an index fund largely depends on the performance of the benchmark index it tracks. The concept of index Funds is not exactly new, the idea came to India in the late 1990s, largely influenced by the success of such funds in the United States and other developed markets. The first index fund in India was launched by UTI Mutual Fund in 1999, named UTI Nifty Index Fund, which aimed to replicate the performance of the NSE Nifty 50 index.

But is there a point in investing in index funds instead of individual stocks or Other mutual funds? Well, one of the most praised advantages of index funds is their cost-effectiveness. The expense ratio: a measure of what it costs an investment company to operate a mutual fund; it tends to be lower for index funds as compared to actively managed funds. This is because index funds are passively managed and require less active trading and research.

Since they are based on indices, they automatically offer diversification across the market, reducing the risk associated with investing in individual stocks. They provide an easy way for investors to gain broad exposure to the market, sectors, or specific segments.

But not everything is well and lovely in the world of index funds, while they can offer cost efficiency and diversification, they are not without limitations. Because they are designed to mimic the performance of an index, they do not aim to outperform the market. Thus, in a rising market, they may not yield as high returns as some of the top-performing actively managed funds.

Additionally, most market capitalization are weighed. This means larger companies make up a more significant portion of the index, and consequently, the index fund. As a result, these funds may be more exposed to the largest companies within the index and may miss out on the higher returns that smaller, faster-growing companies can offer.

Despite that index funds in India present a viable option for investors seeking diversification and cost-effective exposure to the Indian market, like any investment, they come with their own set of pros and cons. Potential investors should consider their individual financial goals, risk tolerance, and investment horizon before deciding whether index funds align with their investment strategy. As always, diversification across various types of investments is recommended.

Let's sum up the advantages and disadvantages of index funds.

Advantages

- Cost-effectiveness
- Diversification
- Transparency

Disadvantages

- Limited Upside
- Market Cap-Weighted Risks

Let's check out a few index funds and what are they all about:

The SBI Nifty Index Fund Direct Plan Growth

This index fund is offered by SBI Mutual Fund that aims to mirror the performance of the NSE Nifty 50 index, representing 50 of the largest and most liquid Indian companies. The "Direct Plan" means investors invest directly with the fund house, avoiding intermediary costs, and typically benefiting from a lower expense ratio. The "Growth" option signifies that any earnings from the fund are reinvested to buy more shares, aiming for capital appreciation over time. As an index fund, it employs a passive management strategy, seeking to replicate the performance of the Nifty 50 index by holding the same securities in similar proportions. Below is the list of the top 10 stocks that they hold in their portfolio. Check out its growth in the last 3 months compared to Nifty 50, as shown in the image below.

Tata Nifty 50 Index Growth Fund

The Tata Nifty 50 Index Fund Growth, offered by Tata Mutual Fund, is an index fund that seeks to mirror the performance of the NSE Nifty 50 Index, pretty much similar to the above index fund. Check out its growth in the last 3 months compared to Nifty 50, as shown in the image below.

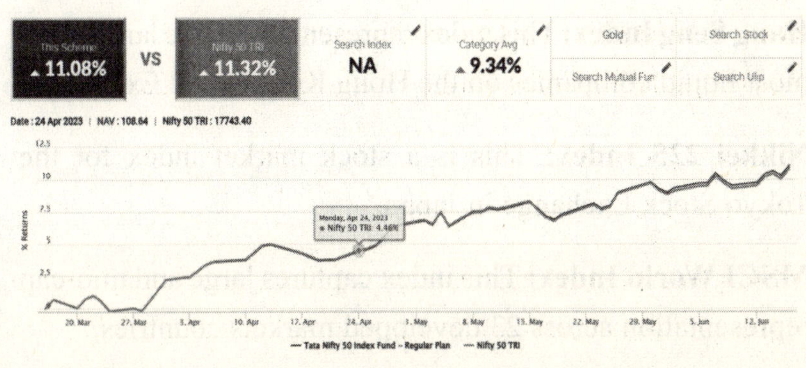

Note: you can also invest in foreign indices apart from the Indian ones. Below is a list of popular indices that Indians can invest in after a thorough analysis.

S&P 500 Index: It tracks 500 of the largest companies listed on the New York Stock Exchange or NASDAQ in the United States. Some mutual funds and ETFs available in India track this index.

NASDAQ 100 Index: This index consists of the 100 largest non-financial companies listed on the NASDAQ stock exchange. Mutual funds and ETFs in India offer exposure to this index.

Dow Jones Industrial Average (DJIA): Known as the "Dow," this index comprises 30 large publicly owned companies based in the United States.

FTSE 100 Index: This index tracks the 100 companies with the highest market capitalization listed on the London Stock Exchange.

Hang Seng Index: This index represents 50 of the largest and most liquid companies on the Hong Kong Stock Exchange.

Nikkei 225 Index: This is a stock market index for the Tokyo Stock Exchange in Japan.

MSCI World Index: This index captures large and mid-cap representation across 23 developed markets countries.

MSCI Emerging Markets Index: This index captures large and mid-cap representation across 26 emerging markets countries.

CHAPTER 9

MANAGING RISK FOR INVESTORS IN THE STOCK MARKET

"The biggest risk of all is not taking one"

- Mellody Hobson

Reading through stock market or financial books, a phrase that often repeats is 'risk-management', and also, it is often the most ignored term. Now that we have talked about where and how you can invest, let's understand how you can save your invested money from probable losses.

You must have heard the line, "Risk hai toh Ishq hai" (If there's risk, there's love). This famous dialogue from Scam 1992 has found its place in the hearts and minds of stock market folks. You might have heard some famous investors say, "I've taken more risks in life than anyone else and if you don't take risks, you can't make big money from the market." Often, stock market related authors, influencers, YouTubers will also tell you that the more risk you take, the more returns you will earn. Higher risk equals higher returns. After hearing all this, you might think that if I don't take risks, I won't make any money at all; I am young, I need to take a lot of risks, I need to buy stocks of small companies that can increase 10 or 20 times. What's the point of investing in large-cap stocks, they only give returns of 10-12%, nothing happens with such low returns.

However, in equity investment, more risk doesn't mean more returns. Yes, it is true that if you are investing, you are taking more risks than FDs, gold, or bonds, and if you don't take more risk than these types of fixed income securities, you won't make more money. But in equity investing, if at one point you take more risk than required, this risk will not give you more returns, instead there is a chance of this risk backfiring. This implies, in actuality, more return is made with less risk.

Suppose you find a penny stock with a market cap of 500 crore, which does a revolutionary business, and you invest in it. After 5 years you realize the company has gone bankrupt and all your money is gone. Instead, if you had invested in a good large-cap or mid-cap consumer stock, which is well-known with an established business model, the stock would have doubled your money in 5 years. People have lost a lot of money in the stock market in the quest of finding hidden gems because they couldn't evaluate its risk. Therefore, by investing, you can earn an extra 2-3% returns just by risk management.

Benjamin Graham provides a great example to explain the concept of achieving higher returns with lower risk. Let's imagine you are selling product X and receive an order for 100 units. The customer informs you that payment will be made only after delivery. Since it's a large order, you decide to accept it. You have two options for sourcing the product: the first place offers it for 60 rupees per unit, while the second place offers it for 50 rupees per unit.

However, there is a risk involved in this transaction. There's a possibility that the customer might refuse to accept the product. Now, let me ask you: from which place would you choose to source the product? Naturally, you would choose the place where you can acquire it for a lower price. When considering this situation in terms of risk and reward, you realize that you can obtain higher returns by minimizing your risk.

If you were to buy from the first place, your risk would be 6000 rupees (100 units * 60 rupees). On the other hand, if you were to buy from the second place, your risk would be 5000 rupees (100 units * 50 rupees). Hence, by opting for second place, you would be exposing yourself to less risk while potentially gaining more reward.

RISK

We've talked a lot about risk, but we haven't defined it yet. In any investment, risk comes from uncertainty, which results in potential financial loss. Risk arises from lack of knowledge, information, and unaccounted factors which can result in financial loss. Risk is both a qualitative and quantitative factor. On one side, where you can measure the risk, the same investment product does not carry the same risk for everyone. Let me explain with an example. Suppose there are two investors, A and B. Investor A is an aggressive and risk-taking individual, while B is a risk-averse investor. If you make A and B invest in a stable low return asset, the situation will be completely different for both of them. For A, the safe investment product is risky because it will yield low returns and the financial goals that could have been achieved quickly by investing in riskier assets will not be achieved and will take time. That means, safe instruments can also be risky for some people based on conditions, while the same product is suitable for B according to his risk appetite. Therefore, the risk rating of every financial product should be according to the risk appetite of each individual, not the same for everyone.

TYPES

Risks are of two types - controllable risk and uncontrollable risk. Controllable risk means those risk factors which were known to you and which you could control or take some action against. Whereas uncontrollable risks are those risk factors which are unknown, which appear due to some unforeseen circumstances and which you couldn't have predicted or controlled at all.

For instance, could you have controlled the crash in the stock market due to the Covid pandemic that occurred in 2020? Could you have controlled the global inflationary pressure that occurred after the war between Russia and Ukraine? Such unaccounted events that increase the risk are uncontrollable risks and you couldn't have countered these things by any means. Now, let's look at the controllable risk in contrast to this.

Suppose you keep only one stock in your entire portfolio and after 5 years, you suffer a 60% loss; you could have controlled this risk by diversification. Let's say you are investing in just one industry and then your portfolio goes down, in this case, you could have controlled this risk. Suppose you are investing in a stock where there is a problem with the management and then your investment becomes zero, here you could have controlled the risk by doing proper research and management analysis. All such risks that you can control or predict are called controllable risks.

Now that we have understood risk well, let's discuss how you can manage risk. Risk management can broadly be done in 5 steps;

Risk Profiling: The first step of risk management involves risk profiling. If you don't know what your risk appetite is, it will be difficult for you to measure and manage risk. Therefore, the first thing you need to do is risk profiling. There are many free websites where you can do this for free.

Diversification: The second step in risk management involves diversification. The examples we discussed in controllable risk can be managed through diversification. List the stocks in your portfolio and check for the factors that can cause volatility in these stocks. If you see many common factors, it means that you need to diversify at a certain level. Diversification should be done according to both stocks and sectors.

Asset Allocation: Asset allocation is a great way to diversify risk. In asset allocation, you invest in negatively related asset classes, which allows you to play out macroeconomic factors well and mitigate portfolio level risk.

Margin of Safety: Let's understand the concept of margin of safety with an example. Suppose a bridge has a capacity of 1000 tons. But the maximum capacity always allowed for this bridge is 900 tons. A margin of safety of 10% is kept so that the bridge does not collapse, i.e., a safety net of 100 tones is kept. Similarly, in investing, if the intrinsic value of a stock is 100 rupees, then you should invest in that stock only when it is trading around 90 if you keep a 10% margin of safety.

Invest for the Long Term: If you are investing, one strategy that will always help you in risk management is long-term investing. The volatility that your stock or asset class is facing due to uncontrollable risk factors gets nullified in the long term. So, if you maintain a long-term relationship with a stock and its fundamentals are right, then you can easily overcome the volatility and build good capital.

I insist to my readers to research and carefully read everything when it comes to making financial choices. India is currently considered as one of the fastest developing countries, with its economy expanding and its markets welcoming foreign investments, as well as becoming self-reliant in numerous ways. If smart financial decisions are made, one is going to experience a wealth boom in the coming years.

"Don't be fearful of risks. Understand them and manage and minimize them to an acceptable level."

— Naved Abdali

CHAPTER 10

PRINCIPLES FOR SUCCESSFUL INVESTING

"The best way to measure your investing success is not by whether you're beating the market but by whether you've put in place a financial plan and a behavioral discipline that are likely to get you where you want to go."

- Benjamin Graham

Throughout this book, we have explored and analyzed investment instruments, examples as well as strategies. In this chapter, I intend to provide you with essential principles that will assist you in solidifying your knowledge, while keeping yourself in check while navigating through this investment journey with confidence.

PRINCIPLE OF LONG-TERM GROWTH:

When it comes to investing, focus on opportunities with strong long-term growth potential. Think of it as nurturing a garden of financial prosperity. Look for companies with sustainable business models, competitive advantages, and solid financials that can blossom over time. Investing in companies with solid foundations can yield significant returns as they thrive and expand. Remember, investing is a marathon, not a sprint. It's not about quick wins or overnight success. As Warren Buffett once quipped, "Someone's sitting in the shade today because someone planted a tree a long time ago."

While the allure of short-term gains may tempt you, it's important to resist the temptation and focus on the bigger picture. As the witty saying goes, "Rome wasn't built in a day, but they were laying bricks every hour." Stay patient, stay committed, and watch your investments grow and thrive, just like the legendary city of Rome.

PRINCIPLE OF THOROUGH RESEARCH

Do not procrastinate on this one. To be a successful investor, it's important to do your homework and research before investing in any company or stock. Take the time to analyze financial statements, understand industry trends, and stay updated on relevant news and events. The more consistent you are with your research, the more you'll learn about the stock market and different businesses. It's not just about numbers, look beyond financial statements and consider qualitative factors like a company's competitive advantage and its management team. This comprehensive approach will give you a better understanding of the company and its prospects.

By staying committed to research, you'll gain insights into market dynamics, economic factors, and industry trends. This knowledge can help you spot opportunities that others might miss and make smarter investment choices. Remember, investing is an ongoing journey and not just a one-day event, the more you learn and research, the more confident you'll become in making informed decisions along the way. So, don't underestimate the power of research. Embrace it as an essential part of your investing strategy, and you'll thank yourself later for the effort you put into expanding your knowledge base.

PRINCIPLE OF DIVERSIFICATION

I cannot emphasize this enough; spread your investments

across different sectors, industries, and asset classes to reduce risk. Diversification is a crucial strategy that helps protect your capital and capture potential opportunities. Think of it as not putting all your eggs in one basket. Instead of investing all your money in a single company or industry, allocate it across various areas. You can invest in different financial instruments, or in different companies, or different sectors. By doing so, you reduce the impact of any single investment on your overall portfolio.

Different sectors and industries thrive at different times. By having exposure to various areas, you increase your chances of benefiting from sectors that are experiencing growth or positive market trends. Keep in mind that diversification doesn't guarantee profits or eliminate the possibility of losses. However, it is a proven strategy to help manage risk and balance your portfolio. The goal is to create a mix of investments that can perform well under different market scenarios.

PRINCIPLE OF PATIENCE

Investing is a long-term game. Don't let short-term market fluctuations push you into making impulsive decisions. It's important to stay focused on your investment goals and have the patience to ride out temporary market downturns. Imagine planting seeds in a garden. You don't expect them to sprout and bear fruit overnight, do you? Similarly, investments need time to grow and flourish. Patience is like the water that nourishes your investment seeds. Sometimes, the market may experience ups and downs, and it's natural to feel a bit anxious. However, if you have followed the previous tips, conducting thorough research and diversifying your portfolio, you have laid a solid foundation for success. Confidence in your investment choices will help you stay patient during market fluctuations.

Remember, impulsive decisions driven by short-term market movements can often lead to regret. Keep your focus on the long-term and resist the temptation to make hasty changes. Stay true to your investment strategy and let time work its magic. It's worth noting that being patient doesn't mean being passive. Stay vigilant and monitor your investments but avoid making knee-jerk reactions based on day-to-day market noise. Trust in your research and the decisions you have made. Over time, patience and a steadfast approach will likely yield better results.

PRINCIPLE OF AWARENESS

Continuously educating yourself about investing is vital. Make it a habit to read books, follow reputable financial news sources, and learn from successful investors. Stay updated by following news channels, media outlets, newspapers, and engaging with other investors and traders. Think of staying informed as sharpening your investment tools. The more knowledge you acquire, the better equipped you will be to make informed decisions.

Moreover, learning from successful investors is like having a mentor guiding you. Study their strategies, understand their approach, and absorb their lessons. Engage with other investors and traders, participate in online forums or communities, and exchange ideas and experiences. These interactions can broaden your perspectives and help you refine your investment skills.

Remember, staying informed is a continuous process. The more you learn, the more confident you'll become in navigating the ever-changing investment landscape. So, make it a priority to continuously educate yourself, absorb knowledge from various sources, and stay connected with the investment community. It's an investment in your own growth!

PRINCIPLE OF CONSISTENCY

Consistency is key in investing. It's important to stick to your investment plan and avoid making frequent changes based on short-term market movements. Remember, time in the market is more important than trying to time the market. Consistency is like nutrition for your financial growth. Just as a balanced diet nourishes your body, consistency in investing nourishes your portfolio. When you deviate from your investment plan by constantly reacting to short-term market fluctuations, you disrupt the steady progress towards your goals.

Trying to time the market, predicting when to buy or sell based on short-term trends, is a challenging task. Even experienced investors find it difficult to consistently make accurate market predictions. By focusing on consistency instead, you shift your attention towards the long-term growth potential of your investments. Additionally, consistency helps you benefit from the power of compounding. Over time, your investments can grow exponentially through the compounding effect, where your returns generate further returns. Consistently investing and staying in the market allows compounding to work its magic and amplify your wealth accumulation.

Whether you're an expert or a beginner in the stock market, keep the above rules or principles in mind. They may seem cliche, and not bear any results in the short term, but later on, you'll thank yourself for putting up with them in the long run!

CHAPTER 11

TOP SECTORAL BETS FOR NEXT DECADE

"You never know what kind of setup market will present to you; your objective should be to find opportunity where risk reward ratio is best."

- By Jaymin shah

I am glad you have finally made it to the last chapter of this book. Until now, we have talked about companies that did well in the past and what were the indications of their growth. However, this book would remain incomplete if I were to leave out the future possibilities. In my opinion, there are a few industries or sectors that have a significant chance to perform really well in the coming years. I have chosen these sectors after a thorough understanding of economic and governmental activities in our country. The government plays a significant role in shaping the economy, and therefore, they come up with various schemes, plans and policies which have a significant impact on industries and sectors. In recent times, the government has been focusing mainly on infrastructure, agriculture, financial services, energy and manufacturing sectors. This has already led to a boom in various industries but considering that India still has a long way to go in terms of strengthening of the economy, there is still a lot more room for these sectors to grow, as suggested by many economic experts. By examining these areas, you can gain a better understanding of where growth might occur next and how you can utilize the same for your own financial growth.

FINANCIAL SERVICES

The first and foremost sector would be financial services. This sector is experiencing tremendous growth in various areas. The financial services sector plays a big role in the overall economy, because financing is crucial for the growth of industries, and the banking sector is a major part of the financial services industry. Private players in the banking sector are performing well for two main reasons. They are good at lending money efficiently, and they are gaining market share from government-owned banks. Private banks are skilled at collecting the money they lend, which helps them reduce the number of loans that are not being repaid. This makes them more profitable compared to government-owned banks, whose non-performing loans are quite high. Managing risks, like non-performing loans, is important for profitability in the lending business.

Another sector in the financial services industry is Non-Banking Financial Companies (NBFCs). NBFCs, especially those involved in consumer loans and housing finance, are also contributing significantly to India's growth.

Insurance companies are also a part of the financial services industry, with two main types: life insurance and general insurance. Additionally, there are companies related to the stock market, such as exchanges, brokerage firms, depositories, and asset management companies.

According to a survey, FinTechs and neobanks are gaining popularity among consumers. People are particularly interested in protecting their data, and traditional banks have an advantage in terms of trust. Some "super apps" may also turn to banks to obtain banking licenses and meet regulatory requirements. Moreover, technological innovations have led to improvements in financial services, especially in digital lending. Overall, this sector is going to see major changes in the coming years.

RETAIL SECTOR

The next big theme in India that investors should not miss is the spending of the Indian middle class. Consumption plays a major role in India's economy, and with a young population and low average income, the spending power of educated and skilled individuals will increase, leading to GDP growth. If you want to invest in the spending habits of the Indian middle class, you can consider looking at large retail companies, consumer goods companies, and the Quick Service Restaurant (QSR) sector.

India is a highly promising market, and many multinational corporations are eager to tap into the Indian consumer base and be the first to enter the market. The increasing purchasing power has created a growing demand. Around 60 new shopping malls with a total retail space of 23.25 million square feet are expected to open between 2023 and 2025. Financial institutions and banks are collaborating with retailers to provide consumers with easy credit options for durable products.

Foreign corporations prefer to invest in India because

of its abundant resources, affordable labor, and incentives such as tax breaks. From April 2000 to September 2022, India's retail trading sector attracted US$4.29 billion in foreign direct investments (FDIs). The Indian government has implemented various rules, regulations, and policies to improve the business environment and make it easier for foreign companies to establish fully owned subsidiaries in India. Hence, this is one sector to keep your eye on.

ELECTRIC VEHICLE INDUSTRY

The next industry is the Electric Vehicle Industry. Conventional Internal Combustion Engine (ICE) cars are going to be replaced by electric vehicles in the future due to their efficiency, advanced features, and most importantly, environmental friendliness. Government support is a major driver in the growth of this industry. The first sector that obviously comes to mind is auto manufacturers. The adoption of EVs is happening the most in 2 and 3 wheelers, so pay more attention to them. The adoption of EVs is also happening in 4 wheelers but at a somewhat slower pace.

The next player in this value chain is EV charging infrastructure companies. However, I have doubts about how much value these companies can create for shareholders. This also includes auto ancillary companies, which make essential automotive parts.

CHEMICALS AND CDMO

Let's talk about two important sectors in Indian manufacturing. First, we have the chemical sector. There are two main reasons for its growth. The United States, a big consumer of chemicals, used to rely heavily on China for their supply. However, now they are looking for opportunities in other countries like India to reduce their dependence on China. Second, due to pollution concerns, the Chinese government has implemented policies to control pollution in the chemical industry. This has affected the production output of Chinese chemical companies and created an opportunity for Indian companies.

Another sector to watch is CDMOs, which stands for Contract Development and Manufacturing Organizations. These companies manufacture drugs for innovator companies on a large scale. Indian CDMOs are the second-largest contract manufacturers globally, after China. They have been successful in gaining market share from Chinese companies. The theme of contract manufacturing in India looks promising for the future, so CDMO companies are worth keeping an eye on.

The demand for specialty chemicals is increasing in industries like food processing, personal care, and home care. This is driving the development of various segments within India's specialty chemicals market. Small and medium enterprises in the domestic chemicals sector are expected to see revenue growth of 18-23% in FY22 due to improved domestic demand and higher chemical prices. Indian specialty chemicals companies are expanding their capacities to meet the rising demand from both domestic and international markets. With global companies looking to diversify their supply chains away from China, the chemical sector in India has a significant opportunity for growth.

The government plans to introduce a production-linked incentive (PLI) scheme to promote domestic manufacturing of agrochemicals. In the Union Budget 2023-24, the Department of Chemicals and Petrochemicals received an allocation of Rs. 173.45 crore (US$ 20.93 million). Foreign direct investment (FDI) inflows in the chemicals sector (excluding fertilizers) reached US$ 20.96 billion between April 2000 and December 2022. In November 2021, Indian Oil Corporation (IOCL) announced plans to invest Rs. 3,681 crore (US$ 495.22 million) to set up India's first mega-scale maleic anhydride unit for manufacturing high-value specialty chemicals at its Panipat Refinery in Haryana. So, I suggest you keep researching and staying updated on this sector.

REAL ESTATE

The real estate cycle in India lasted from 2003-2008 and as soon as the housing bubble burst in America, the real estate sector has been doomed for 12-13 years. But after Covid, tailwinds have started to come back in this sector and there are several triggers for this as well. So, if the real estate sector does well, I believe that its allied sector of building materials will do quite well. Companies that produce wires and cables could also benefit from this growth. In addition, I have seen a revenue growth of 20-25% in piping stocks. Along with this, another allied sector of steel tubes is also seeing a lot of growth where I have seen a few companies already becoming a 10-bagger. So, this is a very interesting sector, and its allied sectors are on my watchlist.

Companies that produce wires and cables, as well as those involved in piping stocks, have shown revenue growth of 20-25%. There is also growth in the allied sector of steel tubes, with some companies experiencing significant growth in their value. These sectors are very interesting and worth keeping an eye on.

According to Savills India, there is a predicted increase in demand for data centers in the real estate sector, expected to reach 15-18 million square feet by 2025. Demand for residential properties has also risen due to urbanization and increased household income. India is among the top 10 markets globally for housing price appreciation. The organized retail real estate stock is expected to grow by 28% to 82 million square feet by 2023.

ICRA estimates that Indian companies are expected to raise over Rs. 3.5 trillion (US$ 48 billion) through infrastructure and real estate investment trusts in 2022. Blackstone, a private market investor, has made significant investments worth Rs. 3.8 lakh crore (US$ 50 billion) in the Indian real estate sector and plans to invest an additional Rs. 1.7 lakh crore (US$ 22 billion) by 2030.

There is a surge in private investment in the real estate sector due to increased transparency and returns. The government has allowed up to 100% foreign direct investment (FDI) for townships and settlement development projects. In the Union Budget 2023-24, a commitment of Rs. 79,000 crore (US$ 9.64 billion) has been announced for the PM Awas Yojana, representing a 66% increase compared to the previous year. Private equity investments in India's real estate sector reached US$ 3.4 billion in 2022, while FDI in the sector (including construction development and activities) totaled US$ 55.5 billion from April 2000 to December 2022.

CAPITAL GOODS

The biggest highlight of this year's budget was the government's push for capital expenditure (capex). If this capex plan plays out well on the government's side, I believe the capital goods sector could directly benefit from it. However, before you consider investing in this sector, remember that capital goods are a deeply cyclical sector and the timing of entry/exit should be perfect, otherwise you could get stuck in them for a long time.

HOSPITAL SECTOR

The final sector is the hospital sector. There are a few reasons for choosing the hospital sector. First, the private hospital sector is greatly under-penetrated in India. Nowadays, any minor or major medical issue in a middle-class family is treated in private hospitals, even though there is a significant under-penetration. As lifestyle diseases are set to rise in India, private hospitals will be a major beneficiary. The second growth trigger in this industry is medical tourism. Medical treatment in India is not only affordable but also of very good quality, which attracts patients from abroad. Most visitors are from Bangladesh, Iran, and African countries, which helps in its growth. Going forward, there are expectations of a 16-17% CAGR growth in this industry, and there is already a lot of foreign investment coming into this sector.

Healthcare market in India is expected to reach US$ 372 billion by 2022, driven by rising income, better health awareness, lifestyle diseases and increasing access to insurance.

In the Economic Survey of 2023, India's public expenditure on healthcare stood at 2.1% of GDP in 2021-22 against 1.8% in 2020-21. In the Union Budget 2023-24, the government allocated Rs. 89,155 crore (US$ 10.76 billion) to the Ministry of Health and Family Welfare (MoHFW). The Indian government is planning to introduce a credit incentive programme worth Rs. 500 billion (US$ 6.8 billion) to boost the country's healthcare infrastructure.

I haven't talked much about particular companies in this chapter because I believe that at this point in the course, you know how companies are analyzed. If any sector seems new to you, read the annual reports of 8-10 companies in that sector to understand its working model. In addition, many consulting firms release industry reports, be sure to read those as well to increase your knowledge of the sectors.

To wrap up, investing in the stock market is a long-term game. It needs patience, careful planning, and understanding of how businesses and markets work. In this book, we've covered a lot of topics to help you make good decisions about your money. But make sure to remember, successful investing isn't about quick wins, it's about growing your money steadily over time. As you keep exploring the world of stocks, keep learning and stay open to new information. The world of investing always has new chances for making money. Use what you've learned here to spot these chances and increase your wealth. Keep going and enjoy your investing journey!

NOTE-

NOTE-